Dean Smith

1931-2015

MORE THAN A COACH

Photographer Hugh Morton made this photograph after Dean Smith won his first NCAA title as UNC beat Georgetown in 1982. Looking spent in this photo following the on-court celebration are (from left) Smith, sports information director Rick Brewer, finals MVP James Worthy and point guard Jimmy Black. (Hugh Morton © North Carolina Collection, U.N.C. Library at Chapel Hill)

This book is available in quantity at special discounts for your group or organization.
For further information, contact:

Triumph Books LLC
814 North Franklin Street
Chicago, Illinois 60610
Phone: (312) 337-0747
www.triumphbooks.com

Printed in U.S.A.
ISBN: 978-1-62937-172-6

The Charlotte Observer
Publisher: Ann Caulkins
Editor: Rick Thames
Book editors: Harry Pickett, Gary Schwab, Bert Fox (photo), Mike Persinger
Lead writer: Scott Fowler
Writers: Frank Barrows, Rick Bonnell, Charles Chandler, Eric Frazier (editorial), Scott Fowler, Ron Green,
Ron Green Jr., Jonathan Jones, Leonard Laye, Max Muhleman, Bob Quincy, David Scott, Jim Utter, Cleve Wootson Jr.
Photographers: David T. Foster III, Davie Hinshaw, Elmer Horton, Jeep Hunter, Diedra Laird, Bob Leverone,
Ozier Muihammad, Gary O'Brien, Christopher Record, Patrick A. Schneider, Jeff Siner
Editorial cartoonist: Kevin Siers
Research: Maria David

Stories are from the Charlotte Observer and also the Charlotte News. The two newspapers merged in 1985.
Dates listed with each story are the dates each story ran in the newspaper.

Content packaged by Mojo Media, Inc.
Joe Funk: Editor
Jason Hinman: Creative Director

Cover Photos
Front cover and back cover bottom left: Observer File Photo/Christopher A. Record
Back cover top left and center middle: Observer File Photo/Bob Leverone
Back cover center right: Observer File Photo/David T. Foster III
Back cover bottom right: Observer File Photo
Back cover top right and center left: Hugh Morton © North Carolina Collection, U.N.C. Library at Chapel Hill

CONTENTS

FOREWORD

By Phil Ford

Coach Smith was my coach and friend for more than 40 years, and I am honestly still trying to get my arms wrapped around his passing. A lot of us are. You probably are, too.

I can tell you that he's really going to be missed. He was such a great man and a guy who always wanted to do what was right. They say we should care for others more than we care for ourselves. You won't find a person on the face of this earth that was willing to help another person more than Coach Smith when that person couldn't repay him in some way.

See, everybody will do something for somebody when they expect to get something back. Coach did things for people and never expected anything back.

Coach Smith was like a second father to all of his former players. I used to kid him all the time that he was the only person I knew who had well over 300 kids. And only four of them — Coach's actual daughters — were girls!

I first met Coach Smith in 1973, when I went to Carolina's basketball camp after my junior year. Later he came to our home in Rocky Mount, N.C., to recruit me. Usually my mom didn't sit in on the recruiting visits — it was just myself, my dad and my high school coach. My mom was a French and English teacher and saw me play basketball in person maybe five times in my entire career. She wasn't a basketball fan. But she sat in on this visit. At first, she thought Coach Smith was actually a dean of some sort at the college.

For the first 30-40 minutes of the conversation, we didn't talk about basketball at all. We talked about being a good citizen, a good friend, a good student. We talked about race relations. And when we finally got into the basketball portion, Coach Smith told me he just didn't know where I would fit in. He said they had a JV program and I might have to play JV some. And I think that's when my mom really fell in love with Coach Smith and became a big fan of his. She knew he would tell the truth.

I wanted to go to North Carolina partly because of Charlie Scott. When he became the first black scholarship basketball player at UNC in the 1960s under Coach Smith, I was in seventh or eighth grade. So you can imagine when all the kids were playing ball in the schoolyard, that's who everybody wanted to be. And it was not just because he was black — it

Dean Smith and point guard Phil Ford, the player who ran Smith's Four Corners offense better than anyone else during his career in the 1970s. Ford became an assistant coach with Smith and the two remained close until Smith's death. (Hugh Morton © North Carolina Collection, U.N.C. Library at Chapel Hill)

was because we all thought Charlie Scott was the best player out there.

I ended up starting at UNC as a freshman, which was a surprise to me. I was terrible at first. I wanted to do well so badly and instead I was dribbling the ball off my foot. One headline read: 'This Ford was an Edsel.' Coach Smith really didn't say anything about it to me, though. And I got better.

Under Coach Smith, everyone got better. You hear people say things like, 'Coach Smith had so much talent and ability on his teams, he should have won more championships.' But they are looking at the finished product. We all were 15-20 times better when we left Chapel Hill than when we first got there.

People say North Carolina has a system. But we don't have a system. We have a philosophy. A system doesn't bend or deviate. A philosophy does. We knew we wanted to play hard, play smart and play together, and we wanted to have fun. But depending on the talent we had, Coach Smith developed different things for us to do offensively and defensively. He gave us a chance to win every game.

Coach Smith was so dedicated to basketball and to his family, but he still found time for social causes. We always knew that side of him, but that's a side he never forced on us. He always just strongly recommended that we get involved with one thing that was very important to us. One cause. One charity. Something. But he wanted us to decide what it was and to do it ourselves.

I went to see him as much as I could for the past few years once I moved back to the Raleigh area. He was still going to his office every

Above: Dean Smith in high school yearbook photo that was taken in 1949 at Topeka High School in Kansas. Opposite: Dean Smith, right, playing for Kansas in 1952. The Jayhawks won the national championship that year. (University of Kansas)

Monday, Tuesday and Wednesday. I'd go by and see him and sit by his desk with him.

Sometimes he would look up and smile. Sometimes he would sleep a lot. I'd sit there sometimes two or three hours with him, and then I would roll him out in his wheelchair to his van and tell him that I loved him.

I'm not sure that he ever knew I was there toward the end.

But I knew I was there.

And in the back of my mind, I would always just hope and pray he would recognize me sitting there, and that he would know I'm sitting there for all the guys who didn't live in the area and couldn't come as often as I did. I was sitting there for all of us, because all of us loved him.

It was hard to do that, of course. You never like to see someone that you love struggle. But a lot of times, that's when they need you the most.

And I do know this. If it had been one of us in that situation, Coach Smith would have been sitting right there. ▪

* *

Editor's note: A three-time All-American during his UNC career from 1974-78, Phil Ford is still No.2 on the Tar Heels' all-time scoring list. He ran Dean Smith's Four Corners better than anyone else ever did, was national player of the year in 1978 and had his No.12 retired by UNC. He later served as an assistant coach for the Tar Heels from 1988-2000. Smith often said "there has never been a guy more loyal to Carolina than Phil Ford."

UNC head basketball coach Frank McGuire and his young assistant coach Dean Smith. (Hugh Morton © North Carolina Collection, U.N.C. Library at Chapel Hill)

Shown here with one of his early teams, Smith preached the importance of taking a good shot so successfully that 32 of his 36 North Carolina squads shot at least 50 percent from the field. (Courtesy of UNC Athletic Communications)

LEGACY OF DEAN SMITH

A COACH WHO FOUGHT FOR WHAT HE BELIEVED WAS RIGHT, NO MATTER THE CONSEQUENCES

By Scott Fowler

In 1984, when I was a freshman at the University of North Carolina trying to get a job as a sportswriter at The Daily Tar Heel student newspaper, I came across an odd question on the application.

"Do you want to meet God?" it asked.

Sure, I thought.

"His office," the application continued, "is in Carmichael Auditorium." The reference, of course, was to UNC basketball coach Dean Smith. By then Smith was a legend, having already guided the Tar Heels to seven Final Fours and one national championship, in 1982.

By the mid-1980s, Smith was 20 years removed from the time UNC students had hanged him in effigy on campus after a loss.

Smith would joke later that he knew the crude figure was modeled on him because of its big nose, and that he was glad the students had "settled for hanging a dummy" instead of the real thing.

Smith had gone on to build and lead a program that was the envy of college basketball, but he always deflected credit for it. One of his former players, a center named David Chadwick who became a well-known minister in Charlotte, once asked if he could get Smith's blessing to write a book about the coach's leadership principles. Smith reluctantly agreed, with one caveat: "Don't deify me."

This book won't do that, either. We will celebrate Smith's life in stories and photos from The Charlotte Observer and The Charlotte News that span his entire career. But there is no need to falsely polish Smith's legend by tweaking the anecdotes to make him sound better.

Dean Edwards Smith was an innovative, caring, socially conscious professor cloaked in the robes of a basketball coach. He did what he thought was right, no matter the consequences. Smith died at age 83 on Feb.7, 2015, surrounded by his wife, Linnea, and his five children and beloved by an extended family of North Carolina players, fans and supporters that stretched around the world. The coach was buried five days later at Old Chapel Hill Cemetery on the UNC campus he so loved.

Charlie Scott (33), Rusty Clark (43) and Dean Smith celebrate after UNC beat Davidson in an NCAA regional in 1968. (Hugh Morton © North Carolina Collection, U.N.C. Library at Chapel Hill)

'TO HIM, EVERYBODY WAS EQUAL'

Frank McGuire, the man a 30-year-old Smith replaced as head coach in 1961, had far more charisma and flash than Smith (and also played more loosely with the NCAA rules). As Billy Cunningham, Smith's first superstar player, once told me: "When McGuire walked into a room, you could sense it. He just had this presence. It's a gift that some people have, and Dean didn't have it. He's not that way. But Dean also made you feel like a person, not just a basketball player. He cared about you long after you left school, and that was whether you were the 12th man or the star."

Cunningham was one of the players who got off the team bus and angrily yanked down Smith's effigy in 1965. Later, Cunningham would become an NBA basketball coach, and he once visited one of Smith's basketball practices in the fall of 1981. Dazzled by the skills of a particular freshman, Cunningham predicted to Smith after the practice that the player — then known as Mike Jordan — would be the best player to ever wear a North Carolina uniform.

"Dean got mad at me," Cunningham recalled. "I tried to calm him down, saying, 'Coach, it isn't brain surgery. Look at him.' Dean didn't like that, though. To him, everybody was equal."

Smith would famously not allow Jordan to appear on the 1981 Sports Illustrated basketball cover with the team's other four starters, ostensibly because he wasn't sure whether Jordan would be the fifth starter or not. Jordan loved Smith and has frequently referred the coach as his

North Carolina coach Dean Smith and South Carolina's Frank McGuire in 1968. Smith succeeded McGuire as Tar Heels coach in 1961, when McGuire left Chapel Hill to coach in the NBA. (Observer File Photo/Elmer Horton)

second father. But he didn't love him that day of the magazine snub.

"That burned me up," Jordan would say in 2009 at his hall of fame induction speech. But it was also a wise psychological move by Smith that fanned the flame of Jordan's competitive drive.

Smith was a master strategist. He enjoyed practices the most — that's where his teaching side came out — and he practiced every late-game situation so often that his players were never surprised by something that happened on-court.

He never cursed. Phil Ford and some of his players laughingly say they sometimes wished Smith did, however, because Smith had other ways of making you feel even worse when you made an error. Smith could "throw chairs with his eyes," as former player Mitch Kupchak once said.

The coach did not run the Tar Heels like a democracy. It was more of a benevolent dictatorship, with Smith firmly in power. He had always liked to be in control, dating back to when he played three high school sports growing up in Kansas. He was a quarterback, a point guard and a catcher. By no coincidence, he called plays or pitches in all three sports.

CRISIS MANAGEMENT

In a crisis, there was no one you would rather have on your side than Smith, either on the court or off. Two quick examples: James Worthy, one of Smith's best players, still remembers the timeout Smith called against Georgetown in the 1982 national championship game, with UNC down by a single point and 32 seconds left in the game.

"The biggest highlight of my college career was that timeout," Worthy once told me.

Think about that for a second. Worthy was one of the greatest players — and finest dunkers — in UNC history. Seconds later, he would make the game-winning steal against Georgetown. But his strongest memory is of a timeout.

"I had never seen Coach Smith so calm," Worthy continued. "I couldn't believe he was so calm. He looked at us with a slight smile, and there was nothing to smile about. I've heard Roy Williams talking about that moment, too — that when he heard Coach Smith talking, he had to fake a cough and then look up at the scoreboard. He thought we were down one point but he wanted to make sure, because Coach Smith sounded like we were up 20. Had it not been for Coach Smith's calm nature, I might not have been able to play the rest of the game very well. I'll be honest — I had just about lost it."

While Jordan made the winning shot seconds later, Worthy had the steal on Georgetown's ensuing possession that clinched the win. Immediately after the game, Smith's first impulse was to find Georgetown coach John Thompson, hug him and console him about the loss. The two were good friends. Smith had once told Patrick Ewing that if he didn't come to North Carolina he should go play for Thompson.

Example No.2: Scott Williams played for Smith from 1986 to 1990. In 1987, in California, Williams' father killed his mother and then killed himself in a murder-suicide. Smith had to break this horrific news to Williams. He went to Williams' dorm-room door in Chapel Hill at 7 a.m.

"I was brushing my teeth and about to head

Dean Smith (front center) celebrates his first ACC tournament championship in 1967 after beating Duke. (Hugh Morton © North Carolina Collection, U.N.C. Library at Chapel Hill)

out the door for an early class," Williams remembered. And my roommate said, 'Coach Smith is at the door. He wants to see you.' I started thinking to myself, 'What have I done wrong?' Because it's not going to be good news if the head coach is at your dorm-room door at 7 in the morning.

"So he told me what happened. And he hugged me. And he gave me an immediate sense that he'd be there to help support me through the process. And he was. So was Coach [Bill] Guthridge. . . . Coach Guthridge accompanied me on my flight home. Coach Smith came to the funeral. I thought that was special. They just didn't put me on the plane with a ticket."

Smith told me years later that he couldn't think of a worse day in his career.

"It was probably the hardest thing I ever did as a coach," he said, "to knock on that door."

PERSONAL STRUGGLES

Smith was not perfect. His first marriage ended in divorce, in large part because at that point in his life he was married to basketball.

The coach could be curt. He could — and did — jab a verbal needle to make a point. He sometimes angered his fellow ACC coaches. Virginia's Terry Holland once owned a dog that he said he named for Smith because the dog whined all night long.

Right: In the late 1960s, North Carolina basketball coach Dean Smith led the Tar Heels to three Final Fours. (Observer File Photo) Opposite: In 1962, Smith's second season, the young coach posed with Yogi Poteet (left) and Billy Cunningham. Nicknamed the "Kangaroo Kid," Cunningham would become Smith's first superstar as a college player. In 1965, Cunningham helped pull down the Smith dummy that UNC students hanged in effigy after a loss. (Courtesy of UNC Athletic Communications)

And Smith's desk was legendarily messy. When you went into his office he had to clear off a chair that was stacked high with a mishmash of papers to find somewhere for you to sit. His assistant coaches knew to never give him anything without keeping a copy for themselves. His longtime administrative assistant Linda Woods was fond of saying that while she kept files, Smith kept piles.

The coach also smoked for decades, often sneaking away like a schoolboy to do so. He finally gave up smoking in 1988, but even then he missed it. Joe Quigg, who played for coach McGuire on the 1957 UNC national title team, once told me about a golf tournament he and Smith participated in that followed Smith's decision to give up cigarettes.

"This young kid came by, threw down a cigarette butt and was about to crush it with his heel," Quigg said. "Dean said, 'No, don't do that. Just let me look at it for a minute.'"

SOCIAL CONSCIENCE

Smith had the heart of a reformer. He had gotten it honestly, from his parents. Alfred and Vesta Smith were public schoolteachers in Kansas, and Alfred also coached almost every sport in high school.

Dean Smith was born in 1931, went to the University of Kansas for college and played sparingly for Phog Allen when the Jayhawks won the national championship in 1952. Even now, in almost every sports gathering in the Carolinas, you can bet somebody there will be able to do a decent Dean Smith impression.

Although he became one of the most well-known men to ever be associated with UNC, Smith was neither a Tar Heel born nor a Tar Heel bred, and after spending his formative years in Kansas that twangy accent never left him.

Smith's family included (from left) his sister Joan Ewing, his father Alfred Smith and his mother Vesta Smith. (Hugh Morton © North Carolina Collection, U.N.C. Library at Chapel Hill)

Smith's sense of social justice began developing early. "Some people have given me kind but undue praise for integrating North Carolina's basketball team in the early 1960s," Smith wrote in his 1999 autobiography "A Coach's Life," referring to his signing of Charlie Scott to be North Carolina's first black scholarship athlete. "My father was the family's true reformer, however. In 1934 he chose to play a black teenager, the son of a janitor who swept the floors at the local bank." Paul Terry played for Alfred Smith's basketball team throughout the regular season, and that squad eventually won a state championship.

Decades later, Alfred's son would help integrate Chapel Hill. First, Smith and his pastor took a black theology student to a restaurant called The Pines that often fed the basketball team but had been a holdout for segregation. The trio ate without incident. Smith would later downplay his role, but how many coaches do you see taking that sort of political stand today?

Then Smith would bring in Scott, who starred for the Tar Heels in the late 1960s and became his most important recruit because his successful career paved the way for Smith to get other talented African-Americans onto his team. Smith never appeared angrier than the night he almost went into the stands in South Carolina, trying to find a fan who kept screaming racist taunts at Scott. (Years later, Scott gave one of his sons the middle name "Dean" to honor his coach).

During his career, Smith would take a stand against the death penalty. He would call the SAT culturally biased. He would campaign for a nuclear freeze. He and his second wife, Linnea (they married in 1976), would criticize Playboy magazine for its objectification of women.

Most of the stands the coach took were liberal. But he also filmed a supportive ad for one of his former players, Republican Richard Vinroot, during Vinroot's ultimately unsuccessful campaign for N.C. governor.

To Smith, loyalty to his former players trumped everything else. Vinroot scored only one point in his UNC career. But when he went to fight in Vietnam, Vinroot got letters once a week from his mother, his wife and Smith.

About the commercial, Smith once said: "We do disagree politically. But I owe Richard. I owe all these guys."

Smith preached academics, and 95 percent of his lettermen graduated.

When the mother of a prime recruit told him her son would fill UNC's gym with fans and implied the player should receive some additional money for doing that, Smith told her that the Tar Heels' arena was already full.

And even if it wasn't, he added, he wasn't going to fill it like that. Needless to say, he didn't get that recruit.

Smith's basketball innovations remain deeply embedded in basketball's and the Tar Heels' culture — the huddle at the free-throw line, the pointing to the player who made the assist, the trapping defense and the Four Corners that was so maddeningly successful it gave birth to the shot clock. He taught his players the value of a good shot so completely that 32 of his 36 UNC teams shot at least 50 percent from the floor.

But Smith lived in the world, not just inside

North Carolina basketball coach Dean Smith is carried by his players after beating Duke in the 1967 ACC tournament finals. (Hugh Morton © North Carolina Collection, U.N.C. Library at Chapel Hill)

the 94 feet of a basketball court.

"He lived by unabashed and solid principles," said Chadwick, who played for Smith from 1968-71. "All those things he hated, like racial segregation, he lived in a way to try to change them."

As he grew older, Smith would wish he had done more. He wished he had scoured the state of North Carolina earlier for black players. He wished he had the opportunity to meet Dr. Martin Luther King Jr., whose quotes Smith often borrowed for his pre-practice "Thought of the Day."

"I look back and see some things left undone," he wrote in his autobiography. "I'm talking about the persistence of things such as social injustice, racial bias, and the continuing struggle to keep college athletics in proper perspective."

THE LAST GOODBYE

Smith coached for 36 years at North Carolina, winning national championships in 1982 and 1993. His consistency was almost mind-numbing. He led the Tar Heels to the Final Four 11 times. Those first three Final Fours, from 1967-69, made sure everyone knew Carolina basketball was relevant again and revived enthusiasm in the program that had been dormant during the early 1960s.

Smith's teams won 20 or more games for 27 years in a row. The Tar Heels finished in the ACC's top three in the regular season for each of the last 33 years of Smith's career. When the coach retired in 1997, at age 66, he had won 879 games — at the time the most any coach had ever won at college athletics' highest level.

And don't forget Smith's international success. With a team that included four Tar Heels, Smith coached the U.S. to the gold medal in the 1976 Olympics after Russia had upset America in a controversial game four years earlier.

The coach's first years in retirement were good years. He enjoyed his children and grandchildren. He watched basketball, usually at home. A lover of golf, he got to play more of it. He relished his role as the Carolina basketball family patriarch, campaigning for his former players to find the jobs they wanted.

His recommendations weren't simply limited to those in Carolina blue, either. Smith gave a strong endorsement to USA Basketball officials for Mike Krzyzewski to take over the U.S. basketball team before the 2008 Olympics.

Both before and during his retirement, Smith attended every big event in his extended light-blue family that he possibly could. Years after Bob McAdoo had left UNC early after playing only one season for the Tar Heels, Smith came to the funeral for McAdoo's wife even though McAdoo had not told the UNC basketball office his wife had died.

Smith's memory was remarkable, allowing him to remember details not only about a person but also about that person's family, job and pets.

But that memory began to fade, slowly, around the mid-2000s.

When I interviewed Smith extensively in 2005 and 2006, his mind was still mostly sharp. But he kept stat sheets, rosters and a UNC media guide close by, because he had started to forget some names and dates.

It wasn't obvious that it was anything more than old age — Smith was in his mid-70s by then. But it was clear his extraordinary mind had

Dean Smith cuts down the net after the 1975 ACC championship win over N.C. State. (Hugh Morton © North Carolina Collection, U.N.C. Library at Chapel Hill)

developed cracks. Smith developed a neurocognitive disorder in the last years of his life. The cruelest irony was that the degenerative disease gradually robbed him of that amazing recall. By the end, due to his dementia, his players had to be reminded to quietly re-introduce themselves to him during his rare public appearances.

Those closest to the coach were heartbroken, caught up in a sad drama that affects millions of American families every year. Many felt they had not had the chance to say a proper goodbye to Smith.

They did get a chance, though, on Feb.12, 2015, at Smith's private funeral at Binkley Baptist Church in Chapel Hill. A number of his former players wore dark suits and Carolina blue ties for the service.

Duke's Krzyzewski wore a Carolina blue tie, too. The outpouring of tributes to Smith after his death came from everywhere. The coach was lauded by everyone from former players to random people he had met on the street to the thousands who had attended his basketball camps to President Barack Obama — who had awarded Smith the Presidential Medal of Freedom in 2013.

They all wanted to honor Dean Smith, the man who was more than a coach. ▧

* *

Scott Fowler is a national award-winning sports columnist with The Charlotte Observer and has worked at that newspaper since 1994. A 1987 graduate of the University of North Carolina, Fowler once served as sports editor of The Daily Tar Heel student newspaper. He has written three books on the history of UNC basketball.

North Carolina coach Dean Smith, left, and South Carolina's coach Frank McGuire, Smith's predecessor at UNC, leave the court — stride for stride — after an ACC game in Columbia, S.C., in 1969. UNC won 68-62. (Observer File Photo/Jeep Hunter)

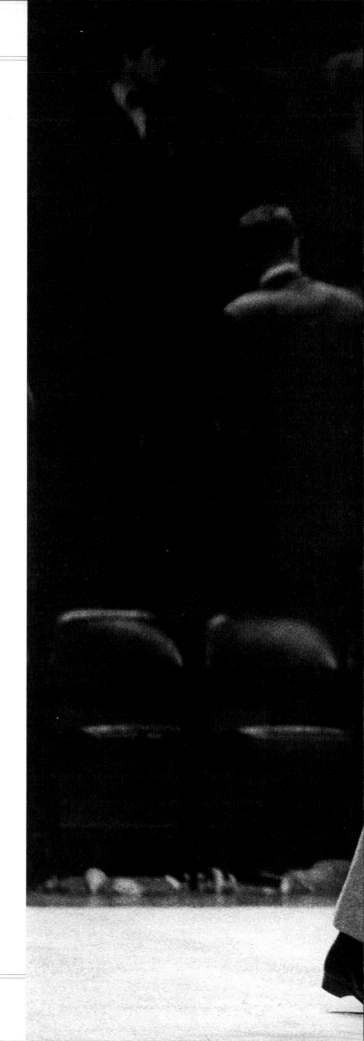

'I'M GOING AFTER IT'

IN 1961, NEWLY HIRED DEAN SMITH
TALKS OF HIS LOVE OF COMPETITION

By Max Muhleman, Charlotte News · August 5, 1961

It was difficult not to think of Dean Smith as the youngest basketball coach stepping into the biggest shoes on the hottest spot.

As Smith stood and allowed the press to gaze upon him for the first time as North Carolina's new basketball coach, Frank McGuire, the man he must replace, was seated beside him.

The dapper fighting Irishman from New York had paid his last respects to all concerned — writers, fans, alumni, the school. He was on his way to Philadelphia and the professional wars. He was making his exit in the Frank McGuire manner — smoothly.

At the same time, his former assistant was making his debut in the Dean Smith manner — exuding bubbling enthusiasm.

When the speeches were over, it was the same.

McGuire in one corner, parrying questions with the dexterity of an accomplished fencer, supplying the correct anecdote at the proper time, dropping a joke when the atmosphere became too somber.

And Smith with his back to the wall, answering everything with the only public relations weapons at his command — a smile and straightforwardness.

It seemed inevitable that eventually the ice would melt. That, the smile on Dean Smith's face would disappear. That Frank McGuire would shake his head sadly and say, "Poor kid. He's got a rough road ahead."

But Smith would not see it so.

"Am I the youngest major college basketball coach in the country?" he began, repeating a question. "I believe there's a fellow at Iowa just a little younger. I'm actually 30, you know, not 29 as some of the stories said. I guess they picked that figure out of last season's brochure."

"What of this youth?" it was wondered. "Do you see it has an advantage?"

"It could never be an advantage," came the surprisingly frank answer. "The more experience you have the better job you can do. But I don't expect my age to be any problem."

"Did you expect to find yourself on one of the Big Four hot seats so quickly when you came here from the West?" it was asked. "Do you find yourself asking now what this is you've gotten into?"

"I like what this is," said Smith. "I love competition. This is tremendous competition. A huge challenge. I'm very happy with the opportunity. I'm going after it the best way I know how." ■

While Smith sometimes hid it well, a fierce competitor burned within him. When he retired in 1997, he had the most wins ever at the highest level of college basketball — 879. (Courtesy of UNC Athletic Communications)

Smith hated to talk about himself in press conferences and would discourage anyone who wanted to do a feature story about him, but he would happily expound on many other topics. (Hugh Morton © North Carolina Collection, U.N.C. Library at Chapel Hill)

A CHALLENGING START

BURNED IN EFFIGY, DEAN SMITH WORKED TO BUILD A STRUGGLING UNC PROGRAM ON PROBATION

By Bob Quincy, Charlotte Observer · March 26, 1982

The request upset Chuck Erickson, North Carolina's athletic director in 1965.

"You know what the basketball coach wants now?" asked Erickson.

Back then, I was the school's sports information director. I shook my head.

"He wants a rug for his office," snapped Erickson. "Can you imagine that?"

What made it worse, according to Erickson, was that the school's basketball team was losing money. Erickson kept close tabs on the athletic department's bank account.

After popping off, Erickson softened and ordered carpeting for Dean Smith's modest little office. In the years since, Smith has compiled a 466-145 record at North Carolina and his Tar Heels will play in the NCAA tournament's Final Four for the seventh time this weekend in New Orleans. His team has made enough money to pay for rugs for every building in Chapel Hill.

I first met Smith at the Final Four in 1957, but remember little about him. He was an assistant coach at Air Force, and he visited North Carolina coach Frank McGuire at his room in the Continental Hotel in Kansas City, Mo.

He and Smith discussed Kansas, the team the Tar Heels were to play — and defeat — in that year's championship game. Smith was slim, polite, soft-spoken. He seemed in awe of the smooth-talking, assured McGuire. "There's one of the brightest young coaches I've met," said McGuire.

A year later, McGuire hired Smith as an assistant. In 1961, when McGuire jumped to the NBA, Smith replaced him. It was a thankless job. North Carolina had been linked to gambling scandals. The Tar Heels were on NCAA probation, their program all but scuttled.

As a result, university president William Friday had taken a stand to de-emphasize basketball by limiting scheduling and recruiting. Smith's first team was 8-9. But he plunged ahead, even though he was seen only as a coach willing to operate a low-key, unambitious program.

The general atmosphere was dark, the campus mood unpleasant. The public acclaimed McGuire, despite the probation he had gotten the school, as a departed genius. Smith was the small-town Kansan holding everything back.

In 1963, Smith got lucky with a 15-6 season, they said. His team featured guard Larry Brown

What about those jackets? In the 1970s, neither Bill Guthridge (left) nor Dean Smith were afraid to experiment with fabric. Guthridge was Smith's assistant for 30 years and then replaced him for three as head coach when Smith retired just before the 1997-98 season began. (Hugh Morton © North Carolina Collection, U.N.C. Library at Chapel Hill)

and center Billy Cunningham. "McGuire's talent," said Smith's detractors. "He can't recruit."

Which was true. Restrictions that had been slapped on the program limited him to signing two out-of-state players annually in those early years.

Smith had to go through some unpleasant moments at North Carolina. After five years, his record was just 66-47. One night in 1965, the team returned from Winston-Salem, where Wake Forest had beaten the Tar Heels. "Burning something down on the lower quad," someone shouted as the team bus arrived at the gym.

Students had set ablaze a cloth dummy that carried Smith's name. The coach didn't blink. He said he'd go see if they wanted to talk. He walked two blocks, faced the crowd in person. He left some friends behind who admired his courage but not his coaching.

Through it all, Smith showed remarkable self-control. With each season, his recruiting became more impressive, especially when the restrictions were lifted. He became a charmer around mothers and fathers.

One spring, he asked me to fly with him and assistant Ken Rosemond to Washington, the home of Bob Lewis, an outstanding high school shooter. From the airport, we took a rental car to Lewis' house.

"This may be difficult," said Smith, noting that schools from coast to coast were pursuing Lewis. Kentucky coach Adolph Rupp had spent three hours in Lewis's home the previous night.

As Smith entered the living room, Lewis casually said, "Where's the paper?" In 1966 and 1967, Lewis was on the All-ACC team.

Eddie Fogler, Dean Smith and Bill Guthridge pose together. Smith was legendary for keeping an untidy desk, and his assistants knew to never give him an important sheet of paper without first making a copy of it for themselves. (Courtesy of UNC Athletic Communications)

In the early years, Smith had to feel his way to establish his coaching technique. The first year or two, he called McGuire after each game. Smith's first superstar was Cunningham, a free spirit who liked to take things upon himself. Cunningham was so good Smith had little choice but to let him play his game.

However, bit by bit, Smith became the Tar Heels' maestro. The most remarkable thing about him is the mental toughness that allowed him to block out the criticism he got in those early years. Some of it bitter and demeaning.

Smith overcame heavy odds to become successful. But to this day, one of his major accomplishments was convincing Erickson to buy that rug for his office. ▦

Above: Sometime in the 1970s, Mildred the Bear "caddying" for (left to right) Bill Guthridge, Larry Brown, Dean Smith at Grandfather Golf and Country Club, Linville, NC. Opposite: An unusual scene - rivals Norm Sloan of N.C. State (left) and Dean Smith (right) sitting together courtside, with UNC assistant coach Bill Guthridge. (Hugh Morton © North Carolina Collection, U.N.C. Library at Chapel Hill)

8 POINTS DOWN, 17 SECONDS TO GO

1974 COMEBACK VS. DUKE BEGAN LEGEND OF DEAN SMITH'S LATE-GAME COMEBACKS

By Charles Chandler, Charlotte Observer · March 2, 1989

There were 17 seconds left and North Carolina trailed Duke by eight points. Fans were leaving Carmichael Auditorium. On the North Carolina bench, coach Dean Smith smiled at his players and said, "Wouldn't it be neat if we could win this game?"

Fifteen years later, Smith still smiles when he thinks about the afternoon of March 2, 1974. When he thinks about the college basketball comeback that has become identified with five words — eight points in 17 seconds.

"Gosh, we were lucky, weren't we?" he said. "You have to be to do what we did."

The Tar Heels scored eight straight points to tie Duke 86-86 in regulation on a last-second, 28-foot shot by freshman Walter Davis, and then beat the Blue Devils 96-92 in overtime.

"It couldn't happen. There's no way it could happen, but it did," says Tony Barone, a Duke assistant coach at the time and now Creighton head coach. "It required everything happening in a perfect, sort of freaky sequence. They did

everything right. Everything that could go wrong for us, did. It still amazes me . . . and it still hurts.

". . . I've got a copy of the film, and I've shown it to the team every year I've been at Creighton. You can tell a kid it's never over till it's over, but those are just words. When you show them proof, it's a lot different.

"Funny thing is, they don't believe it even when they see it."

The game, the last of the regular season, was not expected to be close. North Carolina was 20-4, in second place in the ACC and fourth in the nation. Duke was finishing a season to forget. Head coach Bucky Waters resigned a month before practice began and assistant Neill McGeachy was named interim coach after overtures to former Kentucky coach Adolph Rupp failed.

The Blue Devils had never finished below fourth in the ACC but came to Chapel Hill last, with a 10-15 record. One of the losses was 73-71 to North Carolina in Durham. In that game, Duke had the ball with the score tied 71-71 with four seconds

North Carolina coach Dean Smith, left, and Indiana coach Bobby Knight share a laugh between press conferences in 1981 at the Final Four in Philadelphia. Indiana beat North Carolina in the championship game. (Observer File Photo)

remaining, but Bobby Jones stole an inbounds pass and laid it in at the buzzer.

McGeachy considered suspending more than half the team for the rematch because they were out past midnight the night before attending a streaking exhibition on campus. But he decided against it. The team responded well. Center Bob Fleisher had 17 points and 18 rebounds. Chris Redding scored 18, and Kevin Billerman, now a UNCC assistant coach, had 14 assists. Willie Hodge scored 18 second-half points.

With 17 seconds left, the Blue Devils appeared to have pulled off the upset of the year. They led the Tar Heels 86-78. "I'll never forget seeing the Duke bench about that time," says Ed Stahl, a junior then for the Tar Heels. "They were standing up cheering like crazy. I don't think it ever dawned on them that they might lose."

North Carolina assistant sports information director Rick Brewer had already totaled the minutes played on the official boxscore.

EIGHT POINTS DOWN
Seventeen seconds remained when North Carolina's Jones was fouled trying to rebound a missed shot by Duke.

After a time-out, he faced a one-and-one free-throw opportunity. His season percentage from the foul line was just 60.7. "Bobby Jones was a terrible free-throw shooter," Fleisher says. "I didn't think there was any way he would make them." Jones was perfect twice, cutting Duke's margin to 86-80.

"I don't remember being nervous or confident," Jones says. "What I recall is thinking about the defense we were going to be in if I made them."

Dean Smith walks the floor in Atlanta in the 1977 NCAA final against Marquette and coach Al McGuire (far right). North Carolina lost 67-59. (Hugh Morton © North Carolina Collection, U.N.C. Library at Chapel Hill)

SIX POINTS DOWN

The defense was a zone press.

Stahl, 6-10, was guarding the inbounds passer, Fleisher. Fleisher looked for a teammate for four of the allotted five seconds before attempting to bounce the ball out of bounds off Stahl's legs.

Instead, the ball went between Stahl's legs and into the hands of North Carolina's Davis, who passed to John Kuester for an easy layup. That made it 86-82 with 13 seconds left.

"It was a bad move on my part," Fleisher says. "I blew what should have been an easy way out."

Says Stahl: "Had I been quick enough, I would have tried to deflect the ball with my legs. I've always taken credit for having been too slow. It happened despite me."

FOUR POINTS DOWN

Fleisher's next inbounds pass was lost out-of-bounds by Tate Armstrong, who had cut to the baseline in front of Davis but never gained control of the ball.

"I remember breaking to the basket and not getting the pass immediately," Armstrong says.

The same baseline that was so congested for Duke's inbounds passes was surprisingly open for the Tar Heels. Davis passed in to Stahl, stepped inbounds, got a pass back from Stahl and missed a short jump shot from the right side. Jones rebounded, scored and called a time-out. Suddenly, with six seconds left, it was a two-point game.

TWO POINTS DOWN

Redding, a Duke senior who had watched the two turnovers from the bench, could take no more.

"I basically grabbed McGeachy and told him to put me in for the inbounds pass," said Redding, now a Washington lawyer. "McGeachy didn't tell anybody to come out, so I just picked somebody. I saw Bill Suk and said, 'Billy, you're out, I'm in.'

"When we were in the huddle, McGeachy wasn't saying much except to stay calm and just get the ball in. You've got to remember this was his first year as a head coach. He probably hadn't been in a situation like that before. After all, this was Carolina in Carmichael. There was no play called in the huddle, so I grabbed all the guys and told them what we were going to do. I was determined to get that ball inbounds."

Redding succeeded, passing to Pete Kramer, who was fouled by Kuester. Four seconds remained. Kramer's free throw, the front end of a one-and-one, hit the back of the rim, bounded high and was retrieved by Stahl.

"I didn't feel pressured to make it," Kramer says. "After all, we had a two-point lead with just a few seconds left. I knew it would take a miracle shot for it to go into overtime."

Immediately after Stahl's rebound, with three seconds left, Smith called a time-out. Then McGeachy did the same. When the teams finally took their position, North Carolina's Mitch Kupchak threw to Davis at halfcourt. While Davis was catching the ball, Jones was breaking for the basket.

"Bobby was the decoy," Smith says. "Walter was supposed to have gone down to the foul line extended and shot, but he didn't get that close. "What you've got to remember is Walter wasn't one of the guys they would have thought of. It's hard for us now to think of Walter Davis as a

A typical scene after basketball games for 36 years in the ACC — Dean Smith surrounded by reporters and photographers. (Hugh Morton © North Carolina Collection, U.N.C. Library at Chapel Hill)

freshman with all he's done since. But he hadn't done it at that time."

Davis, unguarded, took three dribbles and launched a 28-foot shot just before the clock ran out.

"It took a long time for that ball to get there. It seemed like forever," says Duke's Hodge, who stood in front of the goal. "I could see it coming, looping, looping. All you could do was wait."

The ball hit the backboard glass and fell through the goal.

"Impossible," Hodge remembers thinking. Carmichael erupted.

"It seemed like a thunderous kind of sound," says Bobby Jones, who played at South Mecklenburg High in Charlotte. "I think that's the loudest I ever heard it in there."

The shot has been called a miracle. Davis, also from South Mecklenburg, says it was an accident. "I didn't try to bank it," says Davis, now with the NBA's Denver Nuggets. "I was definitely trying to swish it in. I never try to use the backboard unless I'm underneath. I wasn't even at an angle. I'm just happy I shot it a little hard."

For that, Redding deserves credit. Redding and Billerman lunged at Davis just before the shot. Redding, at 6-10, got his hand in Davis's face.

"I saw him take a look at me and arc it to get it over me," Redding says. "There's no doubt in my mind that the fact that he put it up a little higher is why it banked in. What a kick in the butt that is."

The Tar Heels fell behind 92-89 in overtime but scored the final seven points to win the game. The fullcourt play Davis scored on is still in Smith's playbook. It's called Duke.

In 1981, Dean Smith appears with three of his starters before the NCAA championship game against Indiana — from left to right, James Worthy, Al Wood and Jimmy Black. The Tar Heels would lose that game to Indiana before winning Smith's first national title the next season. (Hugh Morton © North Carolina Collection, U.N.C. Library at Chapel Hill)

At North Carolina's practice the next day, Davis tried to repeat his shot. "We were joking around and coach Smith said, 'Hey, Walter, let's see if you can do it again,'" Davis says. "He threw me a ball and I shot it from the same spot. It was an air ball."

The comeback left North Carolina fans feeling they were never out of a game, and it earned Smith the label of late-game genius.

"Coach Smith is a master at it," says Kuester, now coach at George Washington. "He made so many good strategic moves that day, but what I'll remember the most about the end is the poise he had and the way he predicted every situation before it happened."

Phil Ford, a current North Carolina assistant coach who began an All- American playing career with the Tar Heels in 1975, says the Duke game had a lasting effect.

"I never give up on North Carolina," Ford says. "So many things have helped fuel that feeling, but nothing more than that Duke game. Because it was so pronounced, being Duke and being on TV, it was like a double fuel to that fire."

Many Tar Heels comebacks followed. In the first round of the 1975 ACC tournament, the Tar Heels trailed Wake Forest 90-82 with 55 seconds left but came back to win 101-100 in overtime. In 1983, North Carolina trailed Virginia 58-42 with 8:43 left, pulled to within 63-53 with 4:12 remaining and then scored the last 11 points to win 64-63.

Smith takes pride in preparing his team to pull off such rallies. He simulates late-game situations at each practice. "I don't believe in drawing up plays in the huddle," he says. "I hope we've practiced it so much that it's already done, so I can just call a play.

"Back in '74 we played an overtime every night at the end of practice. You'd get all kinds of crazy situations."

After 28 years as head coach, Smith admits there has been nothing in practice to match eight points in 17 seconds.

"The best one this year was when we were down 15 with four minutes to play and won by six. Of course, that was with the three-point shot. But eight points in 17 seconds," he says, raising an eyebrow, "that's pretty hard to top."

Barone remembers the humiliation of giving up so many points in so little time and vowed it would never happen to him again.

"That was a very expensive lesson that day for a young coach," Barone says. "What it did was teach me you'd better be totally well-schooled in the out-of-bounds play and you'd better be ready to deal with it in a pressure situation at the end of a game. I can't express that enough. Just ask my team."

Coaches across the country picked up similar lessons. More emphasis was put on preserving time-outs for late-game situations and making opponents win the game at the free-throw line.

"It was on TV, wasn't it?" Smith says. "A lot of things we've done over the years have gotten copied because it's on the tube. It's amazing."

ORIGINS OF A COMEBACK

Dean Smith was about 10 when his father began to teach him the value of being able to come from behind.

The family lived in Emporia, Kan. Alfred Smith was the basketball, football and track coach at Emporia High.

"We started playing ping-pong a lot about that time," Alfred Smith, now 91, recalls. "Of course, I was better than he was. I'd get way ahead of him and then I'd plan to miss a few shots so he could come back and beat me.

"I'd hit the ball too hard so it would go off the end, or hit it into the net, but never so it was obvious to him. I carried him there for several years. I threw a number of games.

"I was trying to prove to him that he could come back and win, no matter what, no matter how far he was behind. Pretty soon, he started believing it. He found out he really could come back. Finally, he got so good, I couldn't beat him anymore."

At 12, Dean Smith won the Kansas state ping pong championship. "I know he claims he let me come back," Dean Smith says now, with a hint of skepticism. "I guess I'll never know."

LASTING LOSS

The defeat lives on for some members of the '74 Duke team.

"You look at teams on TV now that win big games. You see the big celebration on the court, the fans going wild and you realize that could've been us," says Kramer, an insurance executive in Harrisburg, Pa. "I had a feeling it was going to be like this. After the game, I remember saying to someone, 'This is going to be with us the rest of our lives. It won't be something we'll be able to walk away from.' Sure enough, 15 years later . . ."

Fleisher, a surgeon at Duke Medical Center, hasn't forgotten either.

"I'm certainly, at the least, a major contributor to what happened," he says. "That'll stay with me. It doesn't cause me to lose sleep, but obviously I'd like to have it to do over again. I mean, we blew it. We really blew it.

"What bothers me most is we don't have anything athletically to show for that year. It was a difficult season, and that was our one shot that got away. Plus, it would have been really great to have won that game for coach McGeachy. That's something that'll always hurt, I guess."

Neill McGeachy was replaced as Duke's head coach by Bill Foster 26 days after losing to North Carolina. Some have suggested the defeat, and how it happened, cost him his job. Duke's athletic director at the time, Carl James, now commissioner of the Big Eight Conference, says the game had "no impact, either way."

McGeachy spent the next two years as an assistant at Wake Forest, then left coaching. He is now a successful sports promoter.

"I'm really not interested in talking about it," he says when asked about the game. "I've gone on the record about it in the past, for whatever it's worth." Newspaper reports indicate McGeachy had little to say after the game and that he did not allow his players to talk to the media. "Given the 15 years," he says, "I think I've said everything that needs to be said about it."

"Thank you and good night." ◾

Smith calling for the Four Corners was one of the most iconic coaching signals ever. The success of the stall led to the advent of the shot clock in college basketball. (Hugh Morton © North Carolina Collection, U.N.C. Library at Chapel Hill)

WHEN RIVALS CLASH

DEAN SMITH WAS 'RUTHLESSLY COMPETITIVE' AGAINST TERRY HOLLAND, OTHER COACHES WHO CHALLENGED UNC

By Frank Barrows, Charlotte Observer · March 27, 1981

As public figures go, I suppose neither is an especially fascinating case.

One is 38, majored in economics at Davidson, wanted to be a certified public accountant. The second is 50, studied mathematics at Kansas, and hasn't dated Diane Keaton. Both live in quiet college towns. Others in their profession are more flamboyant.

What I find interesting about Terry Holland and Dean Smith is their relationship. I won't call it a rivalry. That is an oversimplification. Better to say a tension exists between them. Holland coaches basketball at Virginia, and Smith at North Carolina.

Their teams meet Saturday in the NCAA tournament's semifinals at Philadelphia. The tension, filtering downward, sets the tone of the game, and, in a sense, explains how two men got there in the first place.

A goodly amount of history is involved. Holland derisively named his dog after Smith. Smith angrily accosted one of Holland's players. Holland has criticized Smith harshly and openly. Smith has lost some tough games to Holland. Holland thinks Smith misuses his power. Smith responds with digs at Holland. He hit me. He hit me first. Now, now, children.

Actually, Holland and Smith are among the most mature and responsible people in their field.

Smith is about to become president of the National Association of Basketball Coaches, and Holland is similarly congenial and decent. Smith reads Kierkegaard and Updike, and Holland likes sailing. Should I have to pick a coach to be marooned on a desert island with, I'd probably select Holland or Smith. Either is pleasant company.

Except if both were on the island, I'd surely get caught in the crossfire. I suppose it all started seven years ago, when Holland arrived at Virginia, where basketball was a sport. Smith, even then, was entrenched at North Carolina, where basketball was, and still is, a religion.

This brought about your basic underdog jealousy on Holland's part. He beat the Tar Heels the second time he faced them. No ACC rookie is supposed to defeat Smith. This drew the lines in the dirt.

In 1976, Holland's squad faced North Carolina in the ACC tournament final. Smith, as the story goes, pushed Virginia's 6-9 Marc Iavaroni while

They weren't always smiling at each other. Pictured here (from left), Virginia coach Terry Holland and Dean Smith, who had an intense rivalry — especially during the Ralph Sampson years in the early 1980s. (Hugh Morton © North Carolina Collection, U.N.C. Library at Chapel Hill)

jogging to the dressing room after the first half. Said Holland: "He told Marc, 'You're a dirty player, and so forth, and so forth.'"

Holland already was sensitized to Smith. During his days as a forward at Davidson, and later as an assistant to Lefty Driesell there, Smith had been the big-school coach who wouldn't schedule the upstart Wildcats. Suddenly, he was the big-school coach who was shoving Holland's players, too.

Anyway, the Cavaliers won that game. Virginia was the conference's sixth-place team, North Carolina had a 25-2 record, and it was an immense upset. The edge between Smith and Holland grew sharper. Smith coached the U.S. Olympic squad the next summer, and Wally Walker, the Cavaliers' star, wasn't originally invited to the tryouts. Holland formed the opinion that Smith, a mover and shaker in basketball politics, uses his influence for his own gain.

Another force was at work, too. In college basketball, games are games. Recruiting, however, is war, and Holland and Smith compete for the same players more frequently than any other ACC coaches. Smith seldom went head to head with N.C. State's Norman Sloan, who focused his recruiting on Washington, and Holland rarely bumps against Wake Forest's Carl Tacy, who concentrates on small-town kids. Smith and Holland aren't that geographically

Right: North Carolina basketball coach Dean Smith looks on during a practice in November 1981. Smith would lead the Tar Heels to a national championship in March 1982. (Observer File Photo/Ozier Muhammad) Opposite: Former North Carolina basketball coach Dean Smith applauds his Tar Heels during the 1982 NCAA championship game in New Orleans against Georgetown. Then-assistant Roy Williams, left, looks on. (Observer File Photo/Davie Hinshaw)

oriented. They're looking for a certain type — the kid who is ultra-intense about the sport.

As a result, they clash.

I don't want to leave out the newspaper article. In 1977, Holland blasted Smith during an interview with a reporter from Richmond, and his comments created a flap. "There is a gap between the man and the image the man tries to project," said Holland. "When I came into this league, I had so much respect for him. I was naïve. . . . Why do I constantly read about a different person from the one I know?"

Plus, Holland's dog was an issue. Or, to be exact, the name of Holland's dog was an issue. Smith complains incessantly to referees during a game. Holland has called his dog "Dean," because, as a puppy, it cried all night. As an inside joke, it was amusing. When Sports Illustrated recently heard, and printed it, nobody laughed.

I'm going to tell you where Smith and Holland insist they stand on the entire matter, and then I'm going to tell you my interpretation. Says Smith: "Terry's wife wrote me a note that she was sorry about the dog thing. I've never really understood. Terry does not know me. My wife knows me, and my golf group knows me. If anybody watched over the years to see who was crying to the officials the most, it'd be interesting."

Clearly, the last is a jibe at Holland. When he rises from the bench, spreads his arms wide to his sides, and puts on his best plaintive look, it's the umpteen zillionth replay of a performance every ACC referee has watched. Says Holland: "I don't have any hard feelings. The only question I have is about the Iavaroni incident."

Despite those disclaimers, the relationship is complex, and less than cordial. I think I know why. Dean Smith and Terry Holland are remarkably alike. Both give considerable thought to their ethics, and both shun celebrity. Both take some pride in their players' academic achievements, and both are quick to point out that basketball is, after all is said and done, merely a game.

Just below that sophistication is their competitiveness. They are healthily and ruthlessly competitive coaches. That is an asset, and yet it is not always attractive. It is, I would venture, even a little scary. They know their intensity, and they know what they've done to control those drives, to limit them.

I believe Dean Smith sees his fierceness in Terry Holland, and Holland sees his in Smith.

I believe it gives them pause, and discomfort. ■

Editor's note: Behind 39 points from Al Wood, UNC defeated a Virginia team led by Ralph Sampson in the 1981 Final Four shortly after this article was published. Then UNC lost to Indiana in the finals.

Former North Carolina coach Dean Smith and then-assistant Roy Williams, left, work the sideline during the 1982 NCAA championship game against Georgetown. (Observer File Photo/Davie Hinshaw)

NATIONAL CHAMPIONS

THRILLING GAME, STARTLING FINISH GIVES DEAN SMITH AN ELUSIVE NCAA TITLE

By Bob Quincy, Charlotte Observer · March 30, 1982

At last, the man is out of shark infested waters. Dean Smith has won an NCAA basketball tournament championship.

North Carolina's 1982 national title was obtained in as thrilling a match as there has been in the 43 years of competition, dating to 1939. And the conclusion of North Carolina's 63-62 victory Monday over Georgetown was downright startling, an Alfred Hitchcock ending.

It was almost like two swordsmen had been dueling — and one dropped his weapon.

Georgetown guard Fred Brown, outstanding in the Hoyas' semifinal victory against Louisville, passed the ball to North Carolina's James Worthy. Five seconds remained and his team was one point down.

Brown was attempting to set up a shot for his team. Worthy's eyes bulged. He couldn't have been more surprised had he been shoved a bag of gold.

Worthy dribbled the ball, was fouled, missed his attempt. What did it matter? Two seconds remained. Georgetown rebounded but missed its 1,000-to-1 chance to make a basket from beyond midcourt.

Bedlam at courtside for North Carolina.

Georgetown appeared stunned. Smith, having attained the goal that made him the complete coach, trotted down the sidelines and hugged opposing coach John Thompson, an old friend who was in shock.

The game was bizarre, thrilling, text book. Smith said he had been outcoached. But his players, particularly forward James Worthy, rose to the occasion.

Scoring 28 points, Worthy made 13 of 17 attempts and must have been in touch with the New Orleans airport tower. He slammed, jammed, rammed and did everything but give a jazz concert before 61,612 . . .

Drained emotionally, Smith was shoved from one microphone to another. He had no chance to savor the most important victory of his life. Normally as composed as an embassy attaché, he wandered a bit.

Not so before the game, when he stopped in the hallway 50 yards behind the playing court and adjusted his tie.

"I'm relaxed," he said smiling. "I hope my players are. We'll find out."

North Carolina basketball coach Dean Smith cuts the net after the Tar Heels defeat Georgetown for the NCAA Championship in 1982 in New Orleans. (AP Images)

Smith was nattily dressed. He wore a dark blue suit, lighter blue striped shirt, dark tie. He didn't give away how much he wanted this one.

Yet, he had feared the worst — and it happened. He might have been cool, but his team looked like Don Knotts in the early going. Its first eight points were courtesy of giant Pat Ewing, Georgetown's 7-foot center, who was playing illegal goaltender.

Even though the Tar Heels got back into the flow, only Worthy was impressive. At the 10-minute mark, North Carolina played a mite better, while the Hoyas looked like hardened veterans. Georgetown led 32-31 at halftime.

Coming out after intermission, North Carolina players huddled about 40 yards from courtside. Maybe they said a prayer. They got better.

Not too much can be said about Worthy's contributions. The team meshed. Freshman Michael Jordan hit the winning basket with 15 seconds left, a soft skyscraper shot from the corner.

And then Brown allowed Worthy to make the immaculate interception. Worthy had no idea anything was coming his way.

As the game ended, Frank McGuire descended from the stands from behind the scorers' table.

McGuire? Remember, he was the man who guided the Tar Heels to their first NCAA championship in 1957. Now he works for Madison Square Garden.

McGuire was smiling.

How do you feel about this one, Frank?

"Just like I did 25 years ago," he said. "Great feeling."

And watching from afar was North Carolina Chancellor Dr. Chris Fordham. Beaming, Fordham used a Lawrence Welk line and said, "Wonderful, wonderful."

Dean Smith reacts on the sideline during the 1982 NCAA championship versus Georgetown. Next to him is assistant coach Eddie Fogler. (Hugh Morton © North Carolina Collection, U.N.C. Library at Chapel Hill)

It was impressive watching the Tar Heels accept their awards. One by one they marched to an elevated stand and shook hands. The Georgetown squad remained at courtside and applauded. Even when the North Carolina manager stepped up. Pat Ewing was applauding, too, and you got the feeling college basketball can be pretty classy at times.

Thompson mentioned the many years of friendship he shared with Smith — and how he knew Smith wanted this championship more than anything.

Thompson also said he wanted to beat his friend for the 1982 championship as much as Smith wanted to beat him. But Smith finally prevailed.

The Tar Heels accomplished quite a bit. They began the season ranked No. 1. They ended the season ranked No. 1 with a 32-2 record. They had played one of the toughest schedules in the country and they won their biggest game in the battle of New Orleans.

Near the North Carolina dressing room stood Tommy Kearns, a muscular, powerfully built 5-10 stockbroker who was a 5-10 guard for the 1957 Tar Heels under McGuire.

"I love this for Dean," he said. "It's a great moment for him and the team. I'm as happy as I was when I played in the big one."

When it was over, Smith could smile. Life was beautiful, no more questions about not being able to handle the crucial test.

Smith politely turned down several requests for national television. He wanted to go home, relax, bask in the knowledge he has done everything expected of a coach. Which he has. ▪

Dean Smith and his five starters pose before the 1982 national championship game against Georgetown. From left to right, James Worthy, Michael Jordan, Dean Smith, Sam Perkins, Jimmy Black and Matt Doherty. Worthy, Jordan and Smith eventually wound up in basketball's hall of fame. (Hugh Morton © North Carolina Collection, U.N.C. Library at Chapel Hill)

UNGUARDED CHAMPIONS

PHOTOGRAPHER CAPTURES POSTGAME MOMENT

By Scott Fowler, Charlotte Observer • June 3, 2006

The starkness of this picture draws you in first. The late Hugh Morton was an environmentalist, a promoter and the best kind of dreamer — the sort who also rolled up his sleeves and went to work.

But it's also important to remember that Morton — who died Thursday at age 85 after a six-month bout with cancer — was a terrific photographer. . . .

My favorite Hugh Morton picture ever? This one. We talked about the photo a few months before his death.

In 1982, Morton took this picture inside the Superdome in New Orleans. The most startling thing about the shot is that it came after North Carolina edged Georgetown, 63-62, in one of the most thrilling NCAA championship games ever.

This was how the Tar Heels looked after Michael Jordan's jumper and James Worthy's steal of Fred Brown's pass — when the world had stopped watching for a moment, but Morton hadn't.

The four men in that cinderblock room look totally spent and lost in their own thoughts.

Photographer Hugh Morton made this photograph after Dean Smith won his first NCAA title as UNC beat Georgetown in 1982. Looking spent in this photo following the on-court celebration are (from left) Smith, sports information director Rick Brewer, finals MVP James Worthy and point guard Jimmy Black. (Hugh Morton © North Carolina Collection, U.N.C. Library at Chapel Hill)

From left to right, that's North Carolina coach Dean Smith, Tar Heels sports information director Rick Brewer, Worthy and Jimmy Black. They are in a holding area, waiting for Georgetown's press conference to conclude. The net draped over Worthy's bowed head is the only indication that North Carolina won the game.

"That's my favorite picture I ever took that included Dean Smith," Morton said several months ago when I talked to him about the picture. "I think it shows a lot of things about him and that night."

Morton, who took pictures of North Carolina sporting events for 60 years, pointed out that Smith's right hand holds a cigarette. Morton said he loved this detail, because it reminded him of Smith's strength of mind.

"It was so hard for him to quit smoking, but he had the determination to do it and then to stick to it," Morton said.

Smith and Morton were longtime friends. I talked to the former Tar Heels coach about this picture a few months ago, too. . . . Said Smith, laughing: "I told Hugh that he didn't have to catch me smoking like that. I've just taken a deep drag, it looks like. I quit in 1988."

Continued Smith: "Sometimes when that photo runs in some publication or the other, the cigarette in my right hand is cut out of the frame. Sometimes you see it. I'm OK with it either way. That's the way we all felt at that moment. Drained.

Thoughtful. You can see it in our faces. It's a true representation."

Brewer is looking at his watch because he wants Georgetown's news conference to end. He is concerned about the deadlines for the reporters at the game and wants to get his crew up on stage for its own news conference.

Morton got this shot not just because he knew Smith. He was hurrying back to the press room after photographing North Carolina's on-court celebration. Then, out of the corner of his eye, Morton saw the room where Smith, his players and PR man Brewer had gathered. Morton told me he scooted in there and started taking pictures before anyone told him not to.

It was great photojournalism — seeing an opportunity, understanding the emotion and capitalizing. ■

Above: All four of the coaches from the 1981-82 UNC championship squad would go on to become head coaches — with three of them becoming the head coach at UNC. From left to right, Roy Williams, Eddie Fogler, Dean Smith and Bill Guthridge. (Courtesy of UNC Athletic Communications) Opposite: North Carolina coach Dean Smith (right) gets a hug from Georgetown coach John Thompson following UNC's win in the 1982 NCAA championship game in New Orleans. (AP Images)

A SECOND CHAMPIONSHIP

ANOTHER WILD FINISH CARRIES NORTH CAROLINA PAST MICHIGAN'S HERALDED 'FAB FIVE'

By Ron Green, Charlotte Observer • April 6, 1993

Dean Smith danced in the Superdome again Monday night, whirling along the sidelines of his floor of dreams in the arms of assistants and players. Danced to the music of cheers for his national champion North Carolina Tar Heels, there in the massive Superdome.

North Carolina had beaten Michigan's heralded Fab Five 77-71 to win the NCAA title and that brief, sudden celebration will be a lasting image because it was Smith finally wearing the mantle of greatness that was rightfully his.

The Tar Heels had won on this same floor in 1982, but one was not enough for some. Now there are two.

Another image that will linger from this magic night for the Tar Heels will be that of Donald Williams standing alone at the foul line with a chance to win the game and millions waiting to see if he would.

He looked so small out there, so young. There were 11 seconds left. North Carolina led by two.

Michigan had been hit with a technical foul for calling a timeout when it had none left and Smith

had crooked his finger at Williams. He made both. Seconds later he made two more.

He scored 12 points in the last seven minutes. And when it was over and the Tar Heels were racing around jumping into each other's arms and pulling on championship caps and smiling and yelping, the vote for MVP was being counted and it was Williams in a landslide.

A TV interviewer pulled Williams in for an interview and teammate Pat Sullivan shouted, "One Shining Moment!" borrowing from a TV theme song.

Williams said this one was for Jim Valvano, the former N.C. State coach who is desperately ill with cancer. "We talked about it at the hotel," said Williams. "He wasn't here and we wanted to dedicate this game to him."

The play that put Williams on the foul line was one of those awful things that appears right out of a nightmare to torture a player or a team down through the years.

Chris Webber, whose physical talent and intelligence were at the center of the Wolverines'

Former North Carolina basketball coach Dean Smith presents the net to his players after the Tar Heels' win against Michigan in the 1993 NCAA championship game. (Observer File Photo/Bob Leverone)

drive to the title game, was trapped in front of his bench and called a timeout. But Michigan had used its timeouts up.

Webber said he didn't remember if anyone had yelled for him to call the timeout but North Carolina's George Lynch later said it sounded like everyone on the Michigan bench was yelling.

The Tar Heels got the free throws, the ball and the victory. And it was so remarkably reminiscent of the 1982 title game, when Georgetown's Fred Brown mistakenly passed the ball to North Carolina's James Worthy, thinking Worthy was a teammate.

But Dean Smith said he didn't think Monday's mistake won the game. He said Webber was trapped, anyway, and might have turned the ball over.

In any case, though, he said, "Say we're lucky, yes. Say we're fortunate, yes. But it still says we're NCAA champions."

Michigan coach Steve Fisher was dumbstruck.

"That's an awful way to have a season end, when you have a chance to get a shot to tie. No one feels worse than Chris but without Chris, we're not here in the first place.

"Regardless of what he or I say, I'm the guy who should have made sure he knew we were out of timeouts."

Now, Fisher will be haunted by this, the way Smith was haunted by the fact that he had won only one NCAA title amid all that glory his teams had accumulated.

North Carolina coach Dean Smith, right, and his Tar Heels watch during the final seconds of a home victory against Florida State in January 1993. Later that season, North Carolina won a national championship. (Observer File Photo/Bob Leverone)

It's a lousy thing to have happen, especially in a championship game. And especially in a game as gripping and well played as this.

This was a game befitting its importance, a game of rising and falling fortunes, of dazzling plays and gritty determination.

Now, North Carolina carries the championship banner back to Chapel Hill. Eight miles away, the past two NCAA banners hang in Duke's Cameron Indoor Stadium.

In the closing moments of North Carolina's victory Monday, Duke coach Mike Krzyzewski was smiling. At least the thing stayed in the neighborhood. It's going to look right at home there. ■

Above: More than 50 years of North Carolina head coaches. From left, Roy Williams, Dean Smith, Bill Guthridge and Matt Doherty when Williams was head coach at Kansas and Doherty was his assistant. (Hugh Morton © North Carolina Collection, U.N.C. Library at Chapel Hill) Opposite: Coach Dean Smith, pointing, and his North Carolina Tar Heels celebrate their victory over Michigan as they're interviewed by CBS's Jim Nantz, left, and Billy Packer in New Orleans, April 5, 1993. (AP Images)

VICTORY NO. 877

TAR HEEL LETTERMEN RETURN TO WATCH SMITH PASS RUPP AS WINNINGEST COACH

By Ron Green, Charlotte Observer · March 16, 1997

He was Dean Smith to the end.

The crowd was chanting "Dean! Dean! Dean!" but he wasn't listening. He was busy, there on the sidelines in his dark suit, his jacket still on, his tie still straight, his eyes darting around the court, as always.

His North Carolina Tar Heels were about to give Smith his 877th victory, one that would move him past Kentucky's Adolph Rupp and make him the all-time winningest Division I coach, but he wasn't thinking about records.

He was coaching.

North Carolina had run away from the Colorado Buffaloes and there were only seconds left in what would be a 73-56 victory in the second round of the NCAA playoffs. He got his subs up and was going to put them in but the regulars were making mistakes and Smith sat the subs back down, not because he was concerned about losing but because he wasn't going to let the regulars rest until they got it right.

With just over half a minute left, he sent in the subs. And while the excitement of this great moment in the history of basketball crackled around Lawrence Joel Coliseum, he was pointing and yelling something to his players, probably about defense.

And then it was over. Smith hurried down the court, shook hands with Colorado coach Ricardo Patton and told him, "We caught you on a bad day."

Dean Smith has caught a lot of guys on bad days. About 877 of them.

He didn't linger to listen to any of the cheers or chants. He hurried off the court toward his locker room, the way he always has. Someone chased him down and dragged him back out for a TV interview. When he went back inside, the hallway was jammed with his former players. A bunch of them had come to honor him on this day to which all of them had contributed.

He loved that, seeing his career layered there in the faces of George Karl and Mitch Kupchak and Bobby Jones and J.R. Reid and Jim Delaney and the others from among his 200 lettermen who could make it back.

"I didn't dream they were all coming back," said Smith. "I don't know how they all got tickets. It was so fun to see them in the hallway.

"That is a special time, as any teacher knows when a former pupil comes back or for a coach when a former player comes back. They always

Dean Smith cuts down the net after the Tar Heels beat N.C. State in the 1997 ACC tournament in Greensboro. Two games later, North Carolina beat Colorado and Smith passed Adolph Rupp for most wins by a Division I coach. (Observer File Photo/Bob Leverone)

say, 'Remember when you got mad at me?' And I always say no.

"I've been fortunate to have some great players, some good players who became better and some who helped the team and didn't play a lot. They all share in this moment, if there is such a thing as this moment."

In the days and weeks leading up to this day, Smith had refused to talk about the record and had resisted any ideas the university had for a ceremony marking the occasion.

Saturday, he relented a little.

He accepted the game ball.

The players had plotted it on the sidelines in the closing moments of the game. When the horn sounded, 7-foot-2 senior Serge Zwikker raced onto the court and snatched the ball out of the hands of a Colorado player. One of the officials in charge of such things pursued Zwikker, asking for the ball and promising to deliver it later to Smith, but Zwikker said, "No, thanks, we'll give it to him."

"This is one I'll take," said Smith, smiling, the tension of the game gone from his face, the burden of the record lifted from his shoulders.

He hadn't put the burden on himself. He had once said he would quit before he broke Rupp's record because he didn't want credit reflected on him that should be given his players and assistants. The record just happened to be there on his way to his 21st appearance in the Sweet 16.

"It never had been a goal of mine, it hasn't been at any point," he said Saturday. "I'm not that type of goal-oriented. We've won 26 games now. We'd like to win 27, and that's my goal."

He talked about his former players, his assistants, the school, the administration, on and on, and concluded, "I'm one of the luckiest guys in the world to be in Chapel Hill and be a coach there."

And vice versa, Coach. ■

North Carolina basketball fans celebrate coach Dean Smith's 877th career victory in Winston-Salem on March 15, 1997. (Observer File Photo/Jeff Siner)

Coach Dean Smith yells instructions during the second half against Colorado during the NCAA tournament in Winston-Salem on March 15, 1997. The Tar Heels won the game, giving Smith his 877th career victory to become college basketball's all-time winningest coach. (Observer File Photo/Jeff Siner)

DEAN VS. COACH K

CALCULATING SMITH, CONFRONTATIONAL KRZYZEWSKI BUILT A RIVALRY THAT PUSHED EACH OTHER TO NEW HEIGHTS

By Ron Green Jr., Charlotte Observer · December 19, 2010

Dean Smith and Mike Krzyzewski can't be measured by numbers any more than music can be defined by notes on a page.

With one more victory, Krzyzewski will tie Smith on Division I college basketball's all-time victories list for coaches. With two more, Krzyzewski will move into second place with only his mentor, Bobby Knight, in front of him, soon to be passed as well.

But to view Smith and Krzyzewski by the numbers is like reading sheet music in a quiet room.

You miss the sound, the fury and the feeling. You miss what Smith and Krzyzewski made of their men and their moments. And you miss how they made us feel watching them work the sidelines, believing anything was possible through will, preparation and teamwork.

There was Smith clapping his hands in frustration or peering out at the court from his seat on the bench, head tilted forward like a man looking over reading glasses. And there was Krzyzewski, sometimes raging with his fists at his side, other times wrapping a hug around a sweaty player's neck.

Their gift is inspiration.

They came from different places — Smith from the plains of Kansas and Krzyzewski from the streets of Chicago — but they went to the same place. The top of their world.

They had their own styles — Krzyzewski more confrontational, Smith more calculating. But beneath the images, the heartbeats were the same. They were driven by success, by excellence and by attention to detail.

They made their players better not just by teaching technique but by instilling self-belief.

They are teachers more than coaches, psychologists of the sideline who understood the value of nuance, preparation and devotion.

Over time, they grew more alike. Krzyzewski once told a friend that if he ever began to act like Smith to please shoot him. Years later, Krzyzewski came to better understand Smith's ways and methods. It was different at the top.

I first met Smith on Dec. 30, 1966, when his Tar Heels played Ohio State in the old Charlotte Coliseum. He was just a few years past being burned

Dean Smith (left) and Duke coach Mike Krzyzewski were fierce rivals for many years. But they eventually became friends, and Smith recommended Krzyzewski to become the U.S. Olympic coach before the 2008 Olympic Games. Krzyzewski wore a Carolina blue tie to Smith's funeral on Feb.12, 2015. (Hugh Morton © North Carolina Collection, U.N.C. Library at Chapel Hill)

in effigy, his North Carolina kingdom still being constructed.

When he shook my 10-year-old hand, it felt like a vice closing around my fingers. Whether he meant to or not, Smith's handshake conveyed power.

He had a remarkable eye for detail and an almost magical recall of names. Smith could meet a person once, not see them for two years, and remember their names when their paths next crossed, often asking about their family, calling them by name, too.

Smith was a master manipulator. We once debated whether a 16-point North Carolina loss qualified as a blowout as I'd termed it in print. A blowout, Smith said, had to be at least 20 points. Always playing the angles.

Above: Duke basketball coach Mike Krzyzewski (center) leaves Binkley Baptist Church following a private church service for Dean Smith in Chapel Hill on Feb. 12, 2015. (AP Images) Opposite: Dean Smith and assistant coach Roy Williams (far right) talk with Michael Jordan and his teammates during a loss to Georgia in the 1983 NCAA regionals. (Hugh Morton © North Carolina Collection, U.N.C. Library at Chapel Hill)

During one of North Carolina's famous comebacks to win a game that seemed certainly lost, he told his team in a timeout huddle to think about how much fun the celebration would be when they won. They were in what seemed an impossibly deep hole late in the game, but Smith was right, the celebration was special.

Krzyzewski's arrival and emergence pushed Smith and ultimately made him better. Krzyzewski was the one ACC coach who never surrendered, who counterpunched and built his program into an empire to match Smith's eight miles away.

I was there the night Duke athletic director Tom Butters gathered the media on campus and announced Krzyzewski as the new basketball coach. Three thoughts crossed almost every mind that night: How do you pronounce it, how do you spell it and who is this guy?

Like Smith two decades earlier, Krzyzewski almost didn't make it. Long before he won four national championships, Olympic gold and commanded rich speaking fees, he was a coach trying to survive.

On some Mondays, local writers would meet Krzyzewski at the Duke golf clubhouse for a pizza lunch. Now, business leaders pay thousands for a few hours of his time.

Both Smith and Krzyzewski have been protective of their privacy. Smith used to hide in tunnels to sneak a final smoke before tip-offs, and his personal life was off limits. He loves good food and golf, playing the maddening game with the same dogged competitiveness he showed on the sideline.

When he felt compelled, Smith would use his pulpit to promote social issues, but he did most of his work quietly, helping to cultivate civil rights and doing small things that felt large to the people he privately helped.

Krzyzewski has chosen his own causes, including a family life center named after his mother, Emily, designed to help people help themselves escape poverty . . .

A couple of years ago when I asked Krzyzewski if he had a few minutes to talk about Smith, who was fighting health issues, he willingly agreed, saying, "I know Coach isn't doing well."

It struck me that Krzyzewski called him Coach, not Dean. It was a compliment.

Krzyzewski talked about what Smith meant to him and to the game they coach, explaining how he had come to appreciate and admire the man he had openly challenged years earlier.

Theirs has been a rare relationship, often as fiery as the rivalry they embody. They have shaped the places they work and the people they've touched. They raised the game and each other. Like no one else. ▪

Known as a great teacher, North Carolina coach Dean Smith works on fundamentals with Mahktar Ndiaye, right, and Antawn Jamison during a practice in January 1996. (Observer File Photo/Bob Leverone)

'I HAVE DECIDED TO RESIGN...'

AFTER YEARS OF PRODDING DEAN SMITH TO KEEP COACHING, HIS EXTENDED FAMILY ACCEPTS IT'S TIME TO WALK AWAY

By Leonard Laye, Charlotte Observer · October 10, 1997

Eddie Fogler knew this time was different for Dean Smith.

"In past years, when he'd call, I'd say, 'Hey coach, you've got to break the record.' We'd tell him, 'We know you're not selfish, but we are. We want to have the record.'"

"The record" came last spring, when the Tar Heels' run in the NCAA tournament left Smith with 879 career victories and eclipsed by three the previous mark established by Kentucky coach Adolph Rupp. The mark, Smith has said, is a tribute to all who have played and coached for him.

"Last year, I said, Coach, break the record, then ride into the sunset. Hi Ho, Silver! and you'll never hear another word from me about it."

Monday afternoon, when Dean Smith invited him into his Smith Center office in Chapel Hill and closed the door, Fogler sensed the coming change.

"Eddie, I just wanted to let you know, I've decided . . ." Smith began.

Fogler interrupted:

"Hi Ho, Silver, coach. You're the greatest!"

Smith laughed. It was a light moment, one of many in the quiet final days before Smith turned a state upside down with news that his unprecedented North Carolina coaching career was at an end.

They were days devoted to basketball and close relationships, spent with players and assistant coaches, past and present. Smith had done this before, countless times. But this week it was different.

After 36 seasons and a career unparalleled in success and personal loyalty as North Carolina's head basketball coach, Smith had decided it was time to step aside.

"By the time the decision came there was no surprise," Fogler said.

This time there was nothing more to say, no more prodding of the man Fogler calls the father of America's largest family.

Fogler, head coach at South Carolina, had sensed it months ago. So had 30-year North Carolina assistant Bill Guthridge, Kansas coach

Dean Smith becomes emotional during a news conference in October 1997, when he announced his retirement as North Carolina's basketball coach after 36 seasons. (Observer File Photo/Patrick A. Schneider)

Roy Williams and one of Smith's closest friends, Bill Miller of Charlotte. Fogler, Williams and Miller had played golf with Smith in Florida in April and saw the retirement coming on an increasingly irreversible path.

Fogler and Williams said they thought about those moments often during Smith's final days on the job, knowing what was coming.

"I had tried to talk him out of it so many times in the past, I wasn't going to try it again," Williams said. "He said to me many years ago that he didn't want to grow old on the bench.

"When he told me it was not emotional — we had already gotten past that point."

Each said the decision had nothing to do with basketball and everything to do with the trappings of the job.

"It's not the coaching that has worn him out," Fogler said. "That's what he thrives on. It's the speaking engagements, the demands of people. . . . There's a message there. . . ."

There was none of that to contend with Sunday night as Fogler, Williams, Appalachian's Buzz Peterson and Middle Tennessee's Randy Wiel arrived in Chapel Hill for their annual fall strategy sessions.

Most of the coaches went to Vinny's Restaurant near Durham for a Sunday night dinner. They were joined by another former Smith assistant, Larry Brown, who brought his Philadelphia 76ers to Chapel Hill for training camp, and Brown's aide John Kuester, another former Tar Heel.

They got a large, rectangular table in a back room and sat in the nearly empty restaurant for almost three hours, having dinner, talking, laughing.

Former South Carolina basketball coach Eddie Fogler, left, and Dean Smith chat before a Tournament of Champions game in Charlotte in 1994. Fogler was a former player and assistant coach for Smith's Tar Heels. (Observer File Photo/Bob Leverone)

Monday morning they met again at the Smith Center, talking shop, drawing plays on a chalkboard.

"When he's at the board, that's his element," Williams said.

"He was excited like he always is when he's talking basketball," Fogler said. "If you had been in that room you'd never have known he was quitting.

"His mind is sharp. I'm not the best X's and O's guy but I'm far from the worst, and I couldn't keep up. I couldn't follow him."

Tuesday brought more of the same. The coaches watched the 76ers practice, then reviewed films of college games. But final decision time was at hand and Smith had to leave for a while, for meetings with university Chancellor Michael Hooker and athletic director Dick Baddour.

Smith returned to the Smith Center and talked to Guthridge, treating this like any other item of business on his calendar.

"It was something real fast," Guthridge said. "He's always in a hurry. I've learned to interpret. He was like, 'Everything went well with chancellor Hooker and Dick Baddour and I think everything is on go.'"

Smith apparently also told his longtime assistant Linda Woods Tuesday.

That night the coaches met again for dinner at Squid's seafood restaurant in Chapel Hill.

"When we got ready to leave I just thanked him, for everything," Williams said. "I said, 'You know what I mean.'"

Wednesday, most of the coaches left town and Smith set the process in motion. Wednesday afternoon, about 4:45, he met with Guthridge and his other assistants, Phil Ford, Dave Hanners and

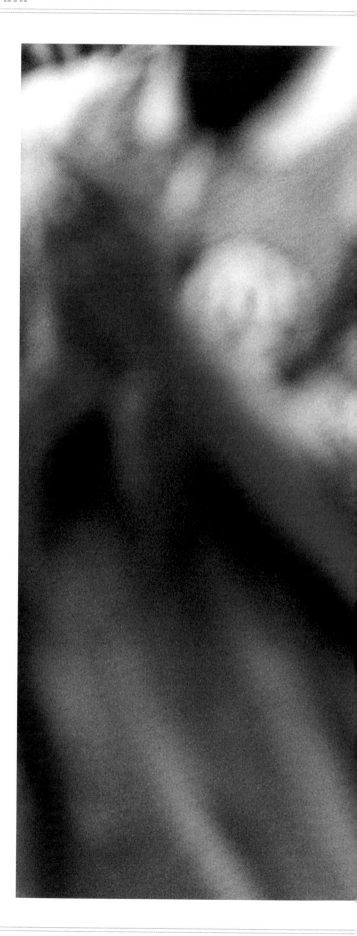

North Carolina coach Dean Smith applauds during player introductions before a game in March 1997. (Observer File Photo/ Bob Leverone)

Pat Sullivan, and the office staff. Most brought note pads, thinking they were having a preseason planning session. "Sullivan, being the newest guy on the staff, thought he was going to get yelled at for something he did wrong," Hanners said.

Everyone found a chair and Smith broke the news, choking up as he did. "It was a bombshell," Hanners said.

Smith apparently wanted to tell everyone individually, but that became impractical. A team photo session was scheduled for 4:45 p.m. in the Smith Center, and Smith joined the team for the pictures. The players then made their preseason mile run at Fetzer Track.

About one hour later the players were asked to gather in the locker room.

Everything seemed normal. Smith was dressed in slacks, dress shoes, a shirt and tie but no jacket. He began by telling the team about some of the tough things he had faced in his life, then began talking about his age.

"I'm 66 now. . . ."

"That's when it hit me," guard Ed Cota said. "I felt a big hit. It was shocking. I couldn't believe it."

Smith went on to tell the team that if he thought he wouldn't have the fire for a season, he would step down. Then he said, "I think that time has come today."

Smith's voice cracked when he told his team Guthridge would be his successor.

No one tried to talk Smith out of it. No one said anything.

North Carolina basketball coach Dean Smith is interviewed after his record-setting 877th victory on March 15, 1997 in Winston-Salem. Smith preferred giving credit for his success to past and present players, including Antawn Jamison, left, and Shammond Williams. (Observer File Photo/Jeff Siner)

Then he went around the room, shaking each player's hand and saying, "Thank you for everything."

"It was tough," forward Vince Carter said. "Everybody broke down. He was looking into everybody's eyes, and he was about to break down. Coaches, managers, everybody was in there, and it was a sad time."

Wrestling with his emotions, Smith left abruptly.

"Those 15 minutes," senior guard Shammond Williams said, "for some of us, it was the worst thing we've ever experienced."

Wednesday night, word gradually began to leak out. Smith called some former players to let them in on his decision.

Thursday morning was routine. There were no flowers or banners or balloons in the office. Former players stopped in to visit with Smith, who made time for them between phone calls.

Among the people who called was President Clinton.

"I let him through," Smith joked.

He thanked Clinton and told the president he had just finished a round of golf with Michael Jordan.

Then at 2 p.m., wearing a blue suit, white shirt and a red pattern necktie, Smith walked to the podium in the Hargrove "Skipper" Bowles room in the Smith Center.

Baddour briefly introduced Smith, who took the microphone and said, "I have decided to resign as head basketball coach."

There was a flash of cameras and silence in the room. ▪

North Carolina basketball coach Dean Smith points to his team as he enters the Smith Center for a news conference on Oct. 9, 1997. He announced his retirement after 36 seasons as the Tar Heels' coach. (Observer File Photo/Jeff Siner)

'I'M TRYING TO DISAPPEAR'

DEAN SMITH TURNS 75, HAPPILY OUT OF THE SPOTLIGHT

By Ron Green Jr., Charlotte Observer · February 28, 2006

Dean Smith turns 75 today and plans to spend his birthday the way he spends most of his days when he's in town.

He'll come to his office deep inside the building named for him, try to work his way through piles of correspondence, chat with Bill Guthridge if his long-time assistant and successor stops into his small office across the hall on his way to the golf course. Then Smith will have a small birthday celebration with his family this evening.

If Roy Williams asks, Smith will stick his head into North Carolina's basketball practice, something he does fairly often, if he doesn't have a conference call or something else on his still cluttered schedule.

"This is my ninth year out of coaching and I don't know where it all went," Smith said Monday morning. "It's gone faster than any part of my life."

Almost a decade since he left the bench, Smith says he has no regrets about when he chose to retire, and is delighted with the state of the program today.

Smith looks good. He has lost some weight, his hair has turned silver-gray and he has been on a regular workout schedule, prompted by Williams.

His office is tucked inside the downstairs administrative offices for the Smith Center. It has no windows and no photos on its walls. The couch and shelves are stuffed with boxes and videos and letters. A cabinet is filled with books and videos. There's a computer and a television beside his desk.

"I like it here," he says. "It's not like upstairs where so many people are coming in and out."

For decades, Smith might have been the most recognizable face in North Carolina. Now he's content to live life in the shadows.

"I'm trying to disappear," he says.

That's why almost two years ago Smith quit doing any public speaking. Other than two clinics a year, one in Europe, one in the United States, Smith stays out of view.

"Corporate speaking is not my cup of tea," he says.

It's one reason he never got into politics despite a deep interest in public policy and government. Years ago, Terry Sanford invited Smith to lunch and suggested the coach run for the U.S. Senate against Jesse Helms.

Smith declined, but Sanford called back and

Dean Smith was there for the news conference in April 2003 announcing Roy Williams as the Tar Heels' new basketball coach. At the urging of Smith, Williams returned to his alma mater after coaching 15 seasons at Kansas, where Smith graduated. (Observer File Photo/David T. Foster III)

asked for another lunch, hoping Smith would reconsider. When Smith mentioned it to his wife, Linnea, "She told me it means two things you hate — cocktail parties and public speaking. It wouldn't have worked at all."

Smith smiles at the memory.

"Plus, I don't think I'd have won," he says.

Smith won 879 games in his 36 seasons at North Carolina, the most in NCAA Division I history. His teams won two national championships, played in 11 Final Fours, made 23 consecutive NCAA tournament appearances and won 13 ACC tournaments . . .

Shortly before the '97-'98 season, Smith announced he was retiring

"Looking back, it was an excellent decision for me and for the program," he says.

"Number one, I knew we'd be a pretty good team. Secondly, I was 66 when I did it and for two or three years before in recruiting, people were always asking me how long I was going to coach. I told them I didn't know but when I (retire) it would be one of these people, Roy Williams, Eddie Fogler, Bill Guthridge or someone from Carolina that would take over.

"I thought I could handle that and I could."

. . . Smith is delighted with the state of the North Carolina program again. In his third season, Williams already has won a national championship and, despite the loss of the top seven scorers from that team, has the Tar Heels in second place in the ACC.

When the Tar Heels came off the court in St. Louis last April, Smith and Michael Jordan were waiting to greet them in the locker room.

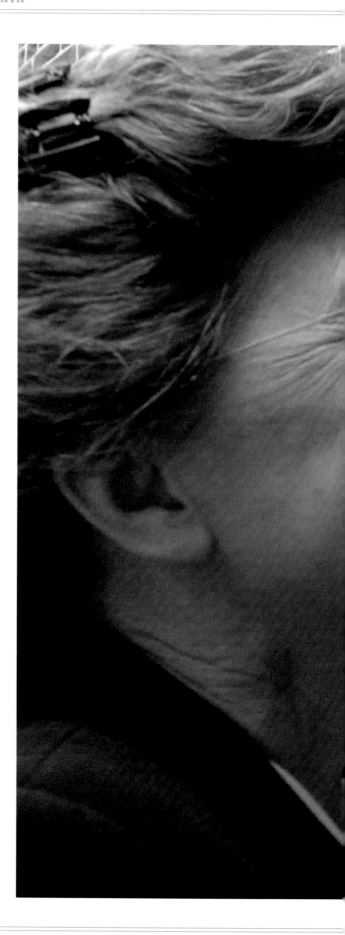

Dean Smith with his wife Linnea in 2006. (AP Images)

Smith reiterated his feeling Monday that winning the national championship "is overrated" because it too often leaves the second-place team and others feeling they didn't accomplish enough.

"But, my gosh, it was exciting," Smith says of the Tar Heels' 2005 title. "I was every bit as happy as I was in 1982."

Smith hasn't often watched the Tar Heels in person since his retirement. He went to Maui with the team in 2004 to play golf with friends, and the only game he's seen in person this season was the opener against Gardner-Webb because it wasn't televised.

He has trouble watching games because he gets nervous.

"I never dreamed I'd experience the nerves I do," he says. "As a coach, you're constantly focusing on the next possession, always thinking ahead. It's terrible just watching. . ."

Smith has five children and six grandchildren. He attends baseball and basketball games his youngest grandson, Brian, plays when he can. He's been to youth soccer games though he admits he doesn't like soccer.

The family makes beach trips together. He took his oldest daughter, Sharon, to Germany last summer so she could return to the place she was born near Munich. Smith sounds like a man who enjoys his life.

Asked if there's something he still wants to do, Smith pauses.

"I could use the old Lou Gehrig line," he says, alluding to his famous farewell speech in Yankee Stadium. "I've been lucky." ▪

Dean Smith in 1985 in the nearly-completed Dean Smith Student Activities Center at North Carolina. UNC played its first game at the Center in January 1986. (Hugh Morton © North Carolina Collection, U.N.C. Library at Chapel Hill)

A PERFECT MOMENT

MICHAEL JORDAN'S KISS SYMBOLIZED ALL DEAN SMITH MEANT

By Scott Fowler, Charlotte Observer · February 9, 2015

The kiss. That is what I remember first when I think about Dean Smith — not the championships, not the Four Corners, not the innovations, not the restaurant integration and not the 879 wins as North Carolina's basketball coach, although all of those were important.

But the kiss was a little more recent, and it symbolized to me how Smith — who died Saturday at the age of 83 — was revered by the UNC community as well as by the world at large.

This was in 2007, in Chapel Hill. The Tar Heels were honoring their 1957 and 1982 national title teams at halftime of a home game. Just before Smith was introduced, Michael Jordan pulled his old coach close, leaned down and briefly kissed Smith on the side of his head as Smith smiled.

It was sweet and perfect, the sort of thing a parent will do to a well-loved child just before something big is about to happen. In this case it was the younger Jordan, towering over his beloved coach.

Then Woody Durham thundered: "Dean Smith!!"

In the building named for him, Smith took a little step forward, lifted both of his hands and then moved them downward, physically trying to tamp down the noise he knew was coming.

No dice. It was one of the loudest ovations I have ever heard.

Anyone of a certain age who graduated from Chapel Hill had some firsthand dealings with Smith. He was omnipresent, a larger-than-life figure, but he tried to deflect attention as much as he could.

One of Smith's many on-court innovations was having a player who scored acknowledge the player who made the pass by pointing at him, and that was what Smith did throughout much of his life. If you turned the attention on him, he would immediately point at somebody else who had helped him get there.

Until a disease robbed him of his memory, Smith's mind was a wonder — a smartphone in the age of typewriters.

"During recruiting, after one visit, he knew the names not only of your parents, but of your siblings, your teammates, your grandparents, your coaches — everybody," former Tar Heel Buzz Peterson said Sunday. "I asked him once how he did it. He said he just concentrated hard during those few seconds of introductions, when most people are worried about saying their own name instead of listening."

All his former players loved Smith, of course.

Michael Jordan gives his former coach, Dean Smith, a kiss during halftime of the North Carolina-Wake Forest game on Feb. 10, 2007. North Carolina's 1957 and 1982 NCAA championship teams were recognized at halftime. (AP Images)

But he treated all people well — not just people who could help him win games.

While she was a student, my future wife served the coach and his family while she was working as a waitress. She still remembers how kind he was to her. As a UNC student myself in the 1980s and then later as a journalist, I saw Smith many times get asked to sign an autograph. He would comply. But he would also sometimes ask the star-struck person on the other end of the pen for their autograph, too.

In our last lengthy interview, which came in 2006 while his mind was still sharp, Smith and I spoke for about an hour in his small office at the Dean Dome before he got tired. We talked about many things, but mostly about that 1982 championship (his first national title as a head coach) because I was working on a book about that season at the time.

Smith recalled the 1982 national title game against Georgetown and Patrick Ewing, still widely considered one of the best games ever played. UNC had the ball and was down by a point with 32 seconds left when Smith called timeout. The first option was to look down low for James Worthy, but Georgetown coach John Thompson knew that and had made sure Worthy was well guarded.

Jordan, a freshman who at the time had such an iffy jump shot he was taking 82 extra jumpers after each practice (82 because it was 1982), would line up on the left wing.

"When we came out of the huddle," Smith said, "I just told Michael: 'If it comes to you, knock it in.'"

Jordan did, swishing a jumper over Georgetown's zone. Jordan still calls that the moment that "Mike Jordan" (as he was known in the 1981-82 UNC media guide) became "Michael Jordan."

Basketball legend Michael Jordan is joined by Dean Smith, his college coach at North Carolina, during Jordan's induction into the North Carolina Sports Hall of Fame December 2010 in Charlotte. (Observer File Photo/David T. Foster III)

It was 25 years later, in 2007, when MJ kissed Smith on the head and gently pushed him in front of the adoring crowd, which was cheering and screaming for the man who had made North Carolina basketball synonymous with excellence.

Smith didn't need the cheers, but the fans needed to do it. They really wanted to kiss or hug the coach themselves. So Jordan — who called Smith his "second father" in a statement Sunday — served as the fans' famous stand-in that afternoon eight years ago.

Like so many millions of people over the years, those fans wanted to tell Dean Smith "Thank you" — not just for winning a lot of basketball games, but for making the world a kinder place. ▪

Above: Former North Carolina basketball coach Dean Smith awaits to be introduced during a ceremony honoring the 2008 ACC Legends. The event was held during the ACC tournament in Charlotte. Opposite: In December 2010, basketball legend Michael Jordan is inducted into the North Carolina Sports Hall of Fame during a ceremony in Charlotte. Jordan receives a hug from Dean Smith, who was his college coach at North Carolina. (Observer File Photo/David T. Foster III)

REMEMBERING DEAN

Remembrances compiled by Rick Bonnell, Scott Fowler, Jonathan Jones, Jim Utter and Cleve Wootson Jr. the day after Dean Smith died.

Jay Bilas, former Duke player and assistant coach under Mike Krzyzewski; current ESPN broadcaster:

"I read his book when I was in my late 20s — 'Multiple Offense and Defense' — and it's still the best book I've ever read about basketball. It's all X's and O's, but it changed the way I looked at the game. I still have my copy, and it has yellow marker all over it.

"Coach Krzyzewski and Coach Smith are similar in more ways than I think people would imagine. When they first started competing, coach Smith was an iconic figure and Carolina was the ACC's gold standard.

"There were things that Carolina and Coach Smith did that rubbed people the wrong way. As Coach K became more established and his program reached that same level of excellence, though, I think he had a greater understanding of all that. Something that might have once annoyed him — he came to realize that, you know what, there was a reason behind all that."

Jeff Lebo, former North Carolina player (1986-89) and now coach at East Carolina:

"The one thing I'll never forget really had nothing to do with basketball. We were in New York City (in November 1988) and I was having

to do some sort of media event with him. I was captain on the team, so the two captains and him we're all in a cab going to this press conference and we pulled up to a red light.

"There was a homeless guy standing on the corner of the intersection. The cab pulled up and coach Smith, who was up front, rolled down his window and took out of his pocket — I don't know how much money it was, but it was substantial — and told the guy to come to the window. He reached his hand out and gave him everything he had in his pocket and told him, 'Please don't use that for alcohol.'

"For me, I was sitting in the back and I didn't know what was going on. I didn't know why he rolled down the window. I didn't know what was happening. That really to me summed up a lot of what coach Smith was about.

"As a player, you remember a lot of things about him, but his compassion toward others and how humble he was were the things that separated him and was special."

Buzz Peterson, member of North Carolina's 1982 championship team and Michael Jordan's roommate:

"In 2001, I was the head coach at Tulsa. Coach was already retired. He wanted our game film all the time, so he could watch us. So I had an

Charlotte Hornets players pause with the Indiana Pacers and the crowd for a moment of silence in honor of Dean Smith before an NBA game on Feb. 8, 2015. Smith died at his home the previous evening. (AP Images)

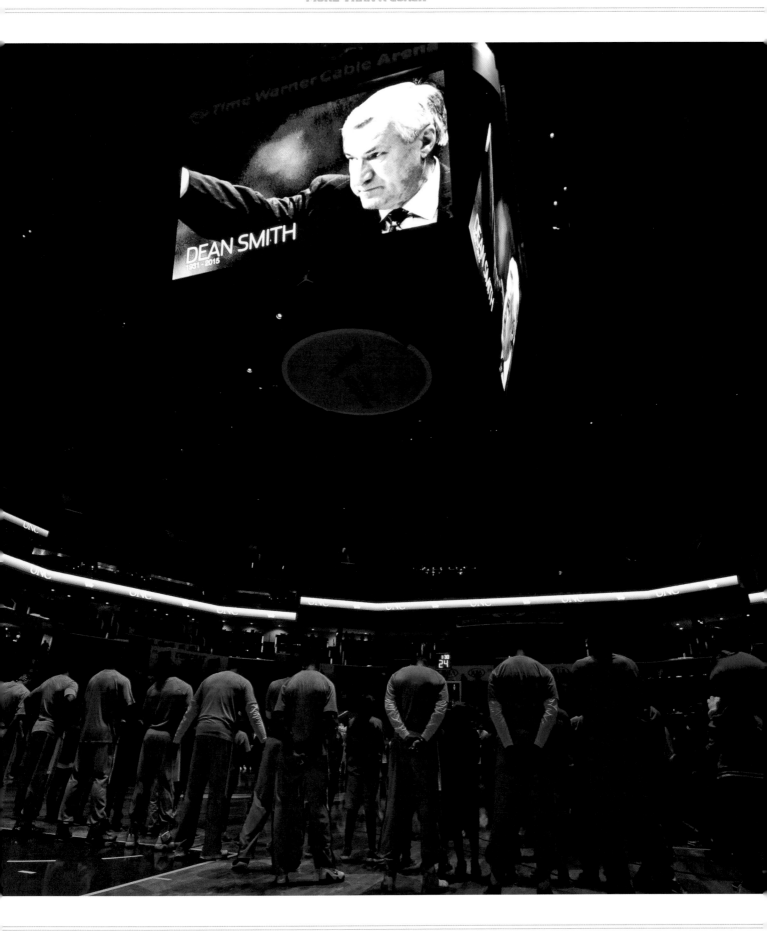

assistant always send it to him. One time he called me right before the NIT and said he was going to send me some ideas we should consider on offense if we wanted to win that tournament.

"I got it a couple of days later — four sheets of paper. It was all sorts of new wrinkles, based on putting four players further from the basket because we had a small team and doing more dribble-drives. We had a good team already. But we won the NIT that year, mostly because of those four sheets of paper."

Al Wood, North Carolina forward 1977-1981:
"When he'd speak to you, he'd make sure to tell you to hug and kiss and take care of your wife and children. That was the most important thing we were ever going to do while we were on the earth.

"That's the thing that sticks with me the most considering I came up without a dad. I had to learn how to be a dad. It wasn't something I was trained at. I didn't know how to do it, and I used to go to him quite a bit."

David Chadwick, player for Smith at UNC from 1968 to '71, senior pastor at Forest Hill Church in Charlotte since 1980 and the author of 'The 12 Leadership Principles of Dean Smith':
"To him, it was always about the team being first. You always pointed to the person who gave you the pass, because the scorer gets the headlines but the person who sacrifices and gets you the ball for the assist does not.

"So you recognize that person — you show the people in the stands and watching on television that person is also important. If you didn't, your rear end would be sitting on the bench next to him.

The ovation for former North Carolina basketball coach Dean Smith was deafening when he was introduced during the ACC basketball tournament in Charlotte in March 2008. Smith was among those chosen for the 2008 ACC Legends class. (Observer File Photo/David T. Foster III)

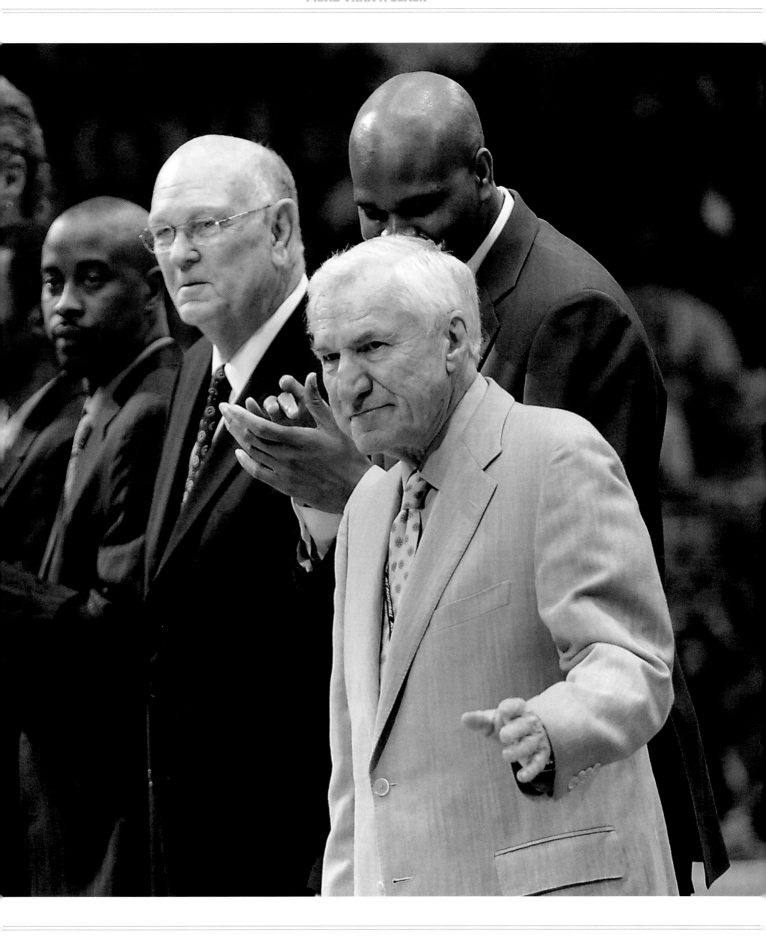

"When someone came out of the game, everyone on the bench had to stand up and applaud, or everyone ran the next day. It was a team game. Everyone was a part of it."

Willie Cooper was the first black player to play on the freshman team at North Carolina:

In 1964 Dean Smith gave Willie Cooper a long-shot chance to be the first black student to play varsity basketball at an ACC school in North Carolina.

Cooper, now 69, played freshman basketball at North Carolina and dealt with many of the indignities black athletes faced in the 1960s. In his sophomore year, he opted to focus on school instead of basketball.

Two years later, Charlie Scott became the first black scholarship athlete at North Carolina.

Cooper said though he didn't play varsity, Smith still treated him like a member of the Carolina family.

"We got to be good friends over the years," he said. " I was just like the other players, I'd go by to see him whenever I went to Carolina."

Cooper graduated from UNC in the spring of 1968 with a degree in business administration, then served in Vietnam. He worked at IBM for 20 years before retiring in 1993. He was responsible for making sure the company's Atlanta regional office hired and promoted minorities.

His son Brent played on North Carolina's 1991-92 junior varsity team.

And in 1994, his daughter Tonya, a sophomore scholarship athlete on North Carolina's women's basketball team, helped the Tar Heels win the national championship.

Dean Smith and Jack Nicklaus share a moment in this undated photo taken in Banner Elk, N.C. Smith loved golf and was a fan of Nicklaus, who sent one of his sons (Jack Nicklaus II) to North Carolina on a golf scholarship. (Hugh Morton © North Carolina Collection, U.N.C. Library at Chapel Hill)

Brad Daugherty, former North Carolina player (1982-86), former NBA star with the Cleveland Cavaliers and now ESPN college basketball analyst and part-owner of JTG Daugherty Racing in NASCAR's Sprint Cup Series:

"When I got to the NBA, coach Smith would always look at what kind of watch I was wearing when I came around — he wanted to make sure I wore a Timex instead of a Rolex. He preached humility."

Walter Davis, who played for UNC from 1973-77 and now works in community relations for the Denver Nuggets:

"I think from the outside everybody knows what a good coach Dean Smith is, but I was even more impressed with the person, from the very first day. He was a good, good man to have on your side. And he treated everybody the same, from Phil Ford — who was the best player on our team — to the guy who made the team as a walk-on."

Charlotte Hornets assistant coach Patrick Ewing, the most dominant high school center of his generation and a player Dean Smith wanted badly at North Carolina:

"When I was on my (recruiting) visit to North Carolina, the words of advice he gave me were if I don't go to North Carolina, I should go to Georgetown because coach (John) Thompson played the position.

"This is a man who could have belittled any of the other coaches from the schools (Ewing considered). Here he takes the opportunity to say if I wasn't going here, then I should go there. That, in my opinion, shows how Dean was a great man."

The Dean E. Smith Student Activities Center opened in 1986. More popularly called the "Dean Dome," it has drawn big crowds — like this one on a rainy day in Chapel Hill — for nearly 30 years. Smith was proud that the building was constructed entirely with private funds rather than any public money. He coached in the building named for him for 11 years. (Hugh Morton © North Carolina Collection, U.N.C. Library at Chapel Hill)

Mark Price, Hornets assistant coach and former Georgia Tech star (1982-86):

Charlotte Hornets assistant coach Mark Price first met Dean Smith as a high school player in Oklahoma. Smith traveled to one of Price's practices, eventually delivering the news that the 6-foot Price just wasn't tall enough to provide what the Tar Heels wanted in a point guard.

The Tar Heels instead signed another Oklahoma high school player, Steve Hale.

Fast forward three years to 1985: Price was then a junior at Georgia Tech, and the Yellow Jackets won both regular-season meetings with the Tar Heels. Then the Yellow Jackets validated that regular-season success by beating North Carolina in the ACC championship game at the Omni in Atlanta.

"After we beat them three times that year, he actually wrote me a hand-written note that congratulated us, obviously, but also said he didn't feel he made a lot of mistakes on the recruiting trail, but I was definitely one of them," Price recalled Sunday.

"He was an incredible class act. He was the standard that everyone was trying to get to in the ACC at that time." ■

Former North Carolina basketball coach Dean Smith leaves the court after a ceremony that honored the 2008 ACC Legends. The event was held during the ACC tournament in Charlotte. (Observer File Photo/David T. Foster III)

COACH SMITH'S FINAL LESSONS

Charlotte Observer editorial, Feb. 9. 2015

Dean Smith made his name as a basketball coach, but his 879 wins and two national championships aren't the only things that made him great.

That's because no one taking the measure of the late UNC-Chapel Hill coach's life can confine his legacy to what he did on the basketball court.

Michael Jordan called him his "second father." President Obama called him "a gentleman and a citizen," a man he was proud to honor with the nation's highest civilian honor, the Presidential Medal of Freedom.

In the wake of Coach Smith's death Saturday at 83, it is entirely proper that we applaud the man who did so much for Tar Heel basketball and the state of North Carolina.

But we should do more than applaud him. As Duke's Mike Krzyzewski pointed out, his greatest gift was "his unique ability to teach what it takes to become a good man."

What, then, can we learn from him as we consider his life?

A few lessons stand out:

* It's not about you — even when it is. Smith was a shy man who deflected praise. He believed he wasn't any better than anyone else, and the team-first approach he taught his players reflected that selflessness. It made his teams stronger units, and his players better men.

* Family isn't just your relatives. He graduated more than 96 percent of his players, and forged such strong bonds with them that he remained in their lives long after they'd left school.

That sense of fellowship — the "Carolina Family," some call it — still binds Tar Heel players across decades and generations.

* Stand up for what you believe in. He helped integrate a Chapel Hill restaurant and recruited Charlie Scott, UNC's first black scholarship athlete. He took stands against the death penalty, for a nuclear freeze and against the lottery.

But his liberal leanings didn't stop him from sticking up for a former player, Richard Vinroot, when the Republican former Charlotte mayor sought his endorsement for governor in 2000.

* Small graces loom large. Smith was legendary for remembering personal details about everyone from star players to bench-warmers and equipment managers. He signed autographs for fans, but sometimes asked for theirs in return. Those small kindnesses left lasting impressions on those around him, reminding them that he cared about them, not just what they could do for him or his program.

So much about sports — and life — boils down to number worship. Who throws the hardest, runs the fastest, jumps the highest, makes the most money.

But Coach Smith's life, ultimately, tells us that's not where greatness lies.

And in our 'selfie'-centered, sports-obsessed society, that's a lesson well worth remembering. ■

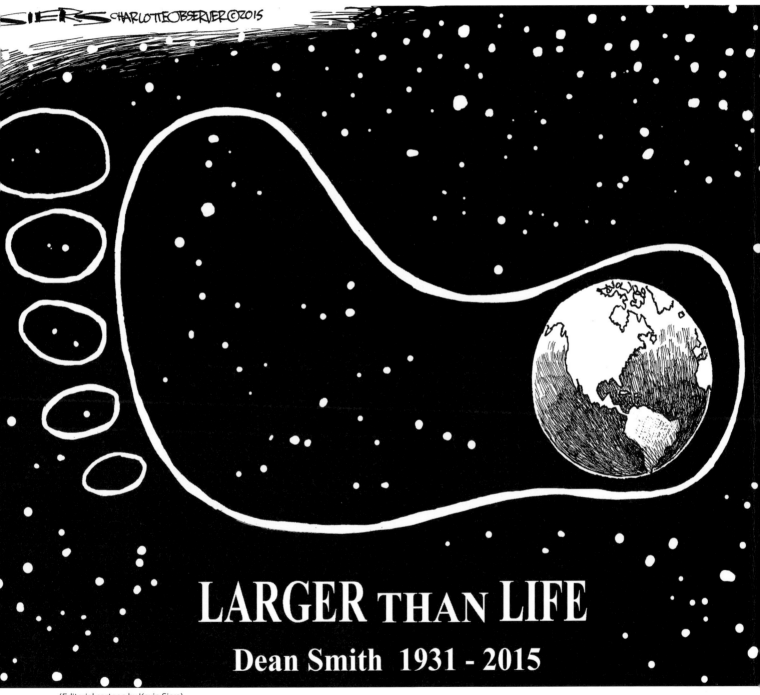

(Editorial cartoon by Kevin Siers)

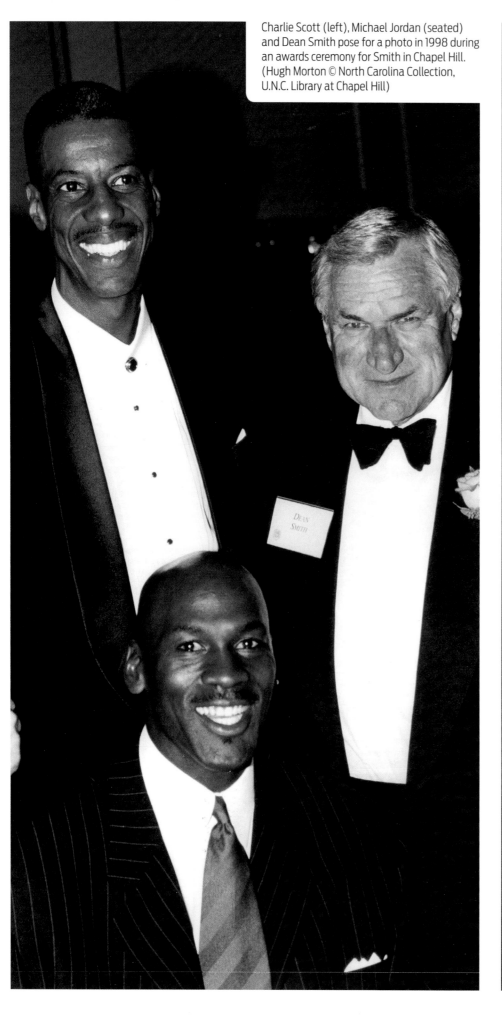

Charlie Scott (left), Michael Jordan (seated) and Dean Smith pose for a photo in 1998 during an awards ceremony for Smith in Chapel Hill. (Hugh Morton © North Carolina Collection, U.N.C. Library at Chapel Hill)

FROM FIRST GAME TO THE END, A FINAL FAREWELL TO DEAN SMITH

By Ron Green, Charlotte Observer · February 9, 2015

It was December 2, 1961. North Carolina's Tar Heels had just won their home opener, defeating Virginia 80-46.

The Tar Heels' new head coach, Dean Smith, met with his team in the locker room, then he came out, looked around at a handful of us who had come looking for a quote or two for our stories and asked Bob Quincy, the sports information director, "What do I do now?"

He figured it out.

When Smith died Saturday night at the age of 83, he left behind 879 victories, including two national championships, 11 Final Four appearances, 13 ACC tournament titles and an image that far outshone even those glowing figures.

I don't know if it's all right to say this, but I feel a sense of relief that he has passed. He was a brilliant man, inside the lines and out, one of the best minds I ever came across in sports, but in recent years his memory had faded. He couldn't remember his great rival Mike Krzyzewski's name.

It was time.

We had what I felt was an ideal relationship for a coach and a sports writer. Friends but not buddies. Respectful. (He would take my calls). Trusting, both ways (he would confide in me, sometimes ask my advice). It's easy to see why his players worshiped him, even long after their playing days.

He was a tough interview, probably because he didn't like the attention.

When he won a milestone game, maybe his 400th or 500th, he would insist that it was significant only in that the Tar Heels had won that game, just another game. And besides, it was the players who had won all those games.

He could be exasperating, but he was consistent at it.

I worked him pretty hard one day when I was interviewing him and Krzyzewski — separately — about the Duke-North Carolina rivalry. Smith kept fending off my questions about his feelings toward Duke.

"Coach," I said, 'Surely you have some kind of strong feelings about Duke,' and he said,

Former North Carolina basketball coach Dean Smith acknowledges the thunderous cheers as he's introduced during the ACC tournament March 2008 in Charlotte. (Observer File Photo/Jeff Siner)

"Well, I don't like their students (the Cameron Crazies). Their language and behavior.'" Nothing about the program.

He didn't like something I said, either. I wrote a column declaring that his Four Corners offense was ruining basketball.

I was in his office a few days later and he motioned toward a thick stack of mail and said, "I've got a letter for you in that stack. I just haven't gotten around to mailing it. It's about your column on the Four Corners. I read what you had to say. I didn't agree with it, but if I agreed with everything you wrote, you wouldn't be doing your job."

Smith had his detractors, starting early. When he was scrambling through the first five years as head coach, never winning more than 16 games and winning as few as eight, some students hanged him in effigy. One wonders how they might feel about that now.

Dean and I played a few rounds of golf together. He could, on occasion, be a brutal needler. But he also could be the guy you'd like to have in your foursome.

Over my years writing sports, I've been accused many times of being biased in favor of North Carolina. I've denied it, saying "I'm in favor of excellence," and I think I've stuck close to that.

But if anyone wants to say I was biased toward Dean Smith, that's OK. He was excellence. ■

Ron Green, 85, is a retired Charlotte News and Charlotte Observer columnist who covered ACC basketball for more than 50 years.

North Carolina coach Roy Williams, Duke coach Mike Krzyzewski (second and third from left) and other coaches and players kneel at midcourt in a moment of silence honoring Dean Smith before the teams played Feb. 18. (Getty Images)

"We honor Dean Smith when we support civil rights for every human being. We honor his memory by never allowing athletics to eclipse academics. And of course every time we enter this building, we will think of Dean Smith, where his remarkable skill and strategy with the game of basketball will never be forgotten."

— **Rev. Robert Seymour,** Smith's longtime minister who also fought alongside Smith for integration in Chapel Hill, speaking to a crowd of about 10,000 gathered Feb. 22 in UNC's Smith Center. At right, coach Roy Williams memorializes Smith with his trademark Four Corners signal.

Observer Photos/David T. Foster III

In December 2010, Dean Smith joined former North Carolina and NBA star Michael Jordan for Jordan's induction into the North Carolina Sports Hall of Fame. Jordan and Smith are watching a video presentation at Time Warner Cable Arena in Charlotte, where Jordan owns an NBA franchise. (Observer File Photo/David T. Foster III)